A Classless Society?

ISSUES

Volume 149

Series Editor

Lisa Firth

 *Independence*

Educational Publishers
Cambridge

First published by Independence
The Studio, High Green
Great Shelford
Cambridge CB22 5EG
England

British Library Cataloguing in Publication Data
A Classless Society? – (Issues Series)
I. Firth, Lisa II. Series
305.5

ISBN 978 1 86168 422 6

Printed in Great Britain
MWL Print Group Ltd

Cover
The illustration on the front cover is by
Don Hatcher.

CONTENTS

Chapter One: Social Class

Chapter Two: Social Mobility

Useful information for readers

Dear Reader,

Issues: A Classless Society?

Some believe old-fashioned elitism no longer has a place in today's society, but is this really the case? A recent poll for the *Guardian* newspaper showed that 90% of 18- to 24-year-olds still feel they are judged by their social class. Has social mobility in the UK come to a standstill? Is so-called 'social engineering' by governments acceptable? How has the rise in graduates affected the UK class system, with more people now identifying as middle class? Is social standing elitist, or a necessary evil of a structured society? These are some of the questions explored in **A Classless Society?**

The purpose of *Issues*

A Classless Society? is the one hundred and forty-ninth volume in the **Issues** series. The aim of this series is to offer up-to-date information about important issues in our world. Whether you are a regular reader or new to the series, we do hope you find this book a useful overview of the many and complex issues involved in the topic.

Titles in the **Issues** series are resource books designed to be of especial use to those undertaking project work or requiring an overview of facts, opinions and information on a particular subject, particularly as a prelude to undertaking their own research.

The information in this book is not from a single author, publication or organisation; the value of this unique series lies in the fact that it presents information from a wide variety of sources, including:
⇨ Government reports and statistics
⇨ Newspaper articles and features
⇨ Information from think-tanks and policy institutes
⇨ Magazine features and surveys
⇨ Website material
⇨ Literature from lobby groups and charitable organisations. *

Critical evaluation

Because the information reprinted here is from a number of different sources, readers should bear in mind the origin of the text and whether the source is likely to have a particular bias or agenda when presenting information (just as they would if undertaking their own research). It is hoped that, as you read about the many aspects of the issues explored in this book, you will critically evaluate the information presented. It is important that you decide whether you are being presented with facts or opinions. Does the writer give a biased or an unbiased report? If an opinion is being expressed, do you agree with the writer?

A Classless Society? offers a useful starting point for those who need convenient access to information about the many issues involved. However, it is only a starting point. Following each article is a URL to the relevant organisation's website, which you may wish to visit for further information.

Kind regards,

Lisa Firth
Editor, **Issues** series

** Please note that Independence Publishers has no political affiliations or opinions on the topics covered in the **Issues** series, and any views quoted in this book are not necessarily those of the publisher or its staff.*

A level playing field

Social and class issues – information from the Association of Graduate Careers Advisory Service

Overview: a class act

'The English class-system is essentially tripartite – there exist an upper, a middle, and a lower class. It is solely by its language that the upper class is clearly marked off from the others ... and a dislike of certain comparatively modern inventions such as the telephone, the cinema, and the wireless' (Mitford, 1956).

When in 1956 Nancy Mitford wrote *Noblesse Oblige* (see above), social class was a relatively straightforward affair. People were born into one of three 'classes' – upper, middle, and lower. Due to the massive economic and cultural disparities, which existed at the time, movement between the classes was rare. But all that was about to change.

The 1960s sent Mitford's class-conscious society into freefall. Post-war economic prosperity, combined with rapid advances in engineering, technology and mass communications, meant that the upper classes were no longer the only ones with money (Clarke, 1997). A new 'classless' society was emerging, epitomised by artists, footballers, politicians and pop stars. In the space of a decade, the world of Nancy Mitford had given way to the world of John Lennon, a world in which being working class was now 'something to be'.

Yet, by the 1970s it was becoming clear that reports of the death of social class had been greatly exaggerated. Britain, it seemed, was still a country in which 'class' was a real, if not always visible factor in shaping people's lives. Numerous sociological studies illustrated the extent to which social class affected where people lived to how healthy they were (Sergeant, 2005). One of these – Paul Willis's classic ethnographic study, 'Learning to Labour' (1978) – was one of the first to trace a link between social class and access to employment opportunities. Willis wrote:

'The difficult thing to explain about how middle class kids get middle class jobs is why others let them. The difficult thing to explain about how working class kids get working class jobs is why they let themselves' (Willis, 1978).

Thirty years on, definitions of 'social class' remain contentious; even so, 'class' remains a key issue when attempting to understand why in society certain groups fare better than others.

Social class and higher education

In 1938, less than two per cent of the 18- to 30-year-old population went to university (Dyhouse, 2002, Redmond, 2004). Today, the figure is 42 per cent . The impact of this is far reaching. In 1910, just 1,000 women were enrolled at UK universities (Schoolnet.co.uk, 2005). Today, women make up 56 per cent of the student population (T.H.E.S., 2005). Mature students (aged 21 and over) now outnumber 18-year-olds.

Big increases have been recorded in the numbers of ethnic minority students, students with disabilities, and students studying on part-time or distance-learning courses.

By the 1970s it was becoming clear that reports of the death of social class had been greatly exaggerated

---

But despite the overall growth in numbers, the proportion of students from the lowest social groups has barely changed in 40 years. Since the mid-1980s, the proportion of people from the poorest 20 per cent of society going to university has risen from 6 to 9 per cent. On the other hand, among the wealthiest 20 per cent the proportion has risen from 20 to 47 per cent (Taylor, 2005). It would seem that university expansion has benefited everyone except the worst off.

Wash 'n' go students

Not only are working-class students less likely to go to university than those from better-off backgrounds, they are more likely to be the first in their families to go to higher education. With less disposable income, above average numbers of poorer students go on to study at local institutions, living at home rather than in halls of residences. Not only is living at home cheaper; it also means minimal lifestyle disruption if a student has a part-time job or childcare commitments.

There is currently no legislation to prevent employers discriminating against applicants on the basis of social class

---

But living at home can also have disadvantages. Recent research has identified the phenomenon of 'wash 'n' go' students – local students whose involvement in higher education is restricted to compulsory engagements such as attending lectures or visiting the university library (Redmond, 2003). 'Wash 'n' go' students have, by definition, limited contact with extra-curricular, socio-cultural aspects of university life – such as participating in student societies or joining clubs. Not only does this pattern threaten to reduce the wider impact of higher education on students' lives, it can also have a negative impact on their long-term career options.

Social class and graduate recruitment

Few employers overtly set out to recruit students from specific social groups (AGR, 2002). However, as the number of students graduating from higher education has increased, many – particularly large firms – have chosen to 'target' their vacancies at specific universities. Rarely are these universities where working-class students are well represented. This has led to the perception that students and graduates from pre-1992

universities enjoy better employment prospects than those from 'new' (i.e. post-1992) institutions (Jethwa and Weir, 2001). According to research, studying at a pre-1992 university can boost a graduate's earnings by between 3 and 6 per cent (Chevalier and Conlon, 2003).

Even if gaining entry to a pre-1992 university, social class still plays a part in determining graduate earnings. Working-class 'Oxbridge' graduates, for example, have been found to earn on average 16 per cent less than 'Oxbridge' graduates from middle-class homes (Conlon and Chevalier, 2000). This has led to the claim that an 'old boys'' (sic) network still exists, particularly in some higher echelons of the graduate recruitment market, with employers continuing to recruit in their own image, rather than simply the most capable (Chevalier and Conlon, 2003).

Understanding the law

There is currently no legislation to prevent employers discriminating against applicants on the basis of social class. This may be because definitions of social class are so problematic. Discrimination, if it does take place, is likely to be indirect e.g. by targeting specific institutions over others, the use of culturally specific interview questions, even the pictures used in graduate recruitment brochures.

Discrimination can also take the form of selection by 'aesthetic skills' (Warhurst and Nickson, 2001) or, to use the sociological term, 'cultural

capital' (Bourdieu and Passeron, 1994). The role of cultural capital in recruitment is well documented (see, for example, Brown and Scase, 1994, Brown et al., 2003, Longden, 2004, Tett, 2000, Warhurst and Nickson, 2001). While everyone possesses different forms of 'cultural capital', it is in the competition for prestigious jobs certain types of cultural capital are likely to assume more symbolic value than others. Critics argue that this is why many graduate recruiters ask questions relating to students' extracurricular achievements – overseas travel, gap years, etc. In one study, for example, it was claimed that while tennis and rowing were taken by recruiters to exhibit energy and contribution, playing snooker did not (Brown and Scase, 1994).

The obvious risk for students from under-represented social backgrounds is that they may be less likely to share the same cultural capital as that prioritised by (middle-class) graduate recruiters. Whether or not this is the case, it is interesting to note how many recruiters still ask for 'that little bit extra' in their recruitment literature – without defining what they take this to mean (Brown and Hesketh, 2004).

By Dr Paul Redmond, Liverpool Hope University

⇨ The above information is reprinted with kind permission from the Association of Graduate Careers Advisory Services. Visit www.agcas.org.uk for more information.

© AGCAS

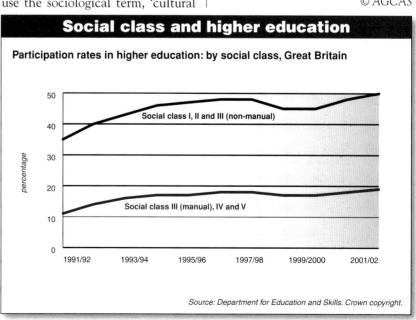

Social class and higher education

Participation rates in higher education: by social class, Great Britain

Social class I, II and III (non-manual)

Social class III (manual), IV and V

Source: Department for Education and Skills. Crown copyright.

Rise of the working class?

March of the middle class slows in the face of 'cooler working class credibility'

There is nothing like class for getting the British all confused. No sooner had the rise of the middle class become regarded as as inevitable as death and taxes, than a majority of the nation reaffirmed its working class roots.

According to the largest survey of social attitudes, published today, nearly six in 10 adults claim to be working class despite the growth in the number of jobs whose pay and prestige would traditionally be regarded as the preserve of the middle class.

The findings of the annual British Social Attitudes survey would appear to undermine the often-quoted claim by John Prescott that 'we are all middle class now'.

But, as always with Britain and class, all is not as it seems.

Staff at the National Centre for Social Research, who questioned 3,000 adults for today's report, said it was remarkable that 57 per cent of those asked claimed they were working class when that figure outstrips the number of people in working class jobs.

The contrast, they suggested, could be because being middle class was seen as 'boring', with people liking to boast they had pulled themselves up by their bootstraps.

Others will label the trend of Britons wanting to be seen as working class, when really they are middle class, as reverse snobbery.

While 57 per cent still maintain they are working class, the number of people happy to declare they are middle class has risen slowly to 37 per cent, from 30 per cent in 1964 and 34 per cent in 1974.

And class remains very important; over the last 50 years there has been no decline in the number of people who identify themselves with a social class.

'The figures are surprising,' said Alison Park, the co-director of British Social Attitudes. 'The number of people who say they are working class outstrips the number of people in working class occupations.

'But people who are socially mobile feel confused and I suspect that, for some people, middle class is seen as slightly boring. A lot of people who are very successful trade on their working class roots and it is more trendy to subscribe to a working class identity.'

She added: 'All of this shows that the idea that class is not important any more is just nonsense.'

Today's report confirms the issue remains as contentious as in 1996 when Mr Prescott, then, as now, the deputy leader of the Labour Party told Radio 4's Today programme: 'I'm pretty middle-class.'

Some disagreed with the former ship steward, including his father.

His remark fuelled a debate over what it means to be middle or working class, and Mr Prescott went back on the show with his father the next day to assure the public he was still in touch with his roots.

Today's survey is based not on jobs but on what class people perceive themselves to be.

It shows that many still regard themselves as working class even if they hold down a job such as an accountant, or manager, because they see their class as something they were born into.

One accountant in London said: 'I belong to the working class because my family are pretty much working class people.'

With the reinvention of the Labour Party as New Labour and the distinction between Left and Right blurred, the report also shows that strong identification with a political party has sharply declined. In 1964 82 per cent strongly identified with a party. By 2005 the figure was only 51 per cent.

Asked whether society was divided by class, many answered without hesitation along the lines of 'yes it is, people either look up or down (at you)'.

Last year a Government report said people employed in jobs associated with middle class pay now outnumbered those in traditional working class roles.

Based on Office for National Statistics' methods, it said that the most common category of worker was 'lower managerial or professional'. This group – including teachers, nurses, actors, police sergeants and journalists – made up 22.4 per cent of all working people.

Another 11.1 per cent came from the top-of-the-tree 'higher managerial and professional' category that took in doctors, lawyers, dentists, professionally qualified engineers and professors. Together the two groups made up 33.5 per cent of all working age people. Only 31.4 per cent were in the job categories most associated with working class pay and conditions.

By Sarah Womack, Social Affairs Correspondent. 26 January 2007

So who do we really think we are?

Information from the Economic and Social Research Council

By Sarah Womack

In the past, it seems, everything was much simpler. We knew which class of society we belonged to and, if not, others would soon tell us. Not any more. The people of Britain are confused over class, as they are over race and gender issues. We are more uncertain about our place in society than ever before, as Sarah Womack reports.

The issue of identity has never been more complex. In a fast changing society, it is difficult for people to know where they belong. Take John Prescott. He caused a flurry of excitement in 1996 when he declared 'we are all middle class now' – (that's class pronounced 'classse', not 'clarse').

His father Bert, a retired railwayman, was having none of it. 'John worked as a steward on ships serving drinks to well-to-do passengers', Bert Prescott told *The Sun*. 'If that's not working class, I don't know what is.'

This was a silly spat but Mr Prescott has always been class conscious, not least because his first job was indeed as a steward on the Cunard line. His servile status in that job is regularly referred to by 'toff' Tory MP Nicholas Soames, who shouts across the Commons floor: 'A whisky and soda for me, Giovanni. And a gin and tonic for my friend.'

But it is not just the deputy Labour leader who is confused.

Research by Professor John Curtice, of the University of Strathclyde, and Professor Anthony Heath, of the University of Oxford – *Are Traditional Identities in Decline?* – for the ESRC's Identities and Social Action Research Programme found that the middle classes are now the muddle classes.

The vast majority, 57 per cent, said they were working class, twice the number of people actually in occupations associated with working-class pay and conditions (which is

31.4 per cent, according to the Office for National Statistics). A straw poll by *The Daily Telegraph* found people redefining class for themselves.

Sir John Mortimer, the barrister, writer and dramatist, declared: 'I'm profoundly middle class. I was the son of a barrister and became a barrister myself. It would be terrible to consider yourself upper class and I thought the working class had been abolished.'

> **In the past, it seems, everything was much simpler. We knew which class of society we belonged to and, if not, others would soon tell us**

Lady Antonia Fraser, the historian and daughter of Lord Longford, said she belonged to the 'Bohemian class'. It was left to Ben Fogle, the TV presenter and writer, to sum up the confusion, saying: 'I am always referred to as middle class and in a way I am, having had a privileged upbringing and been privately educated. But our class system is not as defined as it used to be, with a lower, a middle and an upper class. There are many more categories now.'

As Professor Curtice points out, modern society means identity is fragmented. 'The character of class identity may well have changed, as evidenced both by an apparent decline in its association with attitudes and in changed understandings of what makes someone middle or working class,' he says. But he and Professor Heath cautioned: 'A decline in the incidence of a particular social

identity does not necessarily mean that its individual level influence has declined or that people are free to "choose" their identities.'

It is not just class which confuses, but race and even gender. What, for example, does it mean nowadays to be British in a multi-cultural society? Two-thirds of the population state that multi-culturalism makes Britain a better place to live but no one who watched *Big Brother* could have missed the abuse hurled by Jade Goody at Bollywood actress – and eventual winner – Shilpa Shetty. Many commentators suggested class was also involved. Miss Shetty was middle class while Jade has been held up as the archetype of the white working class. The racist outburst came as a bit of a shock in 21st-century Britain which prides itself on young people from different cultural groups 'rubbing along'.

Professor Margaret Wetherell, director of the ESRC programme, points out: 'Britain has a lively (and economically beneficial) "tikka masala" culture. The large majority of Muslims report strong identification with (and pride in) both Britain and Islam and citizens of UK cities are more likely than any other European country to describe foreigners as well-integrated into their cities.'

Britain does indeed boast a respect for cultural diversity and tolerance – 'a convivial culture' – which makes it an attractive place to settle. It has, as Professor Wetherell says, become a 'highly integrated and in some ways a more capacious, less overtly racially prejudiced and parochial society'. At the same time, Miss Goody's antagonistic views were virtually endorsed by two other *Big Brother* contestants and Channel 4 declared the show a 'mirror of society'.

Another area for identity confusion is parenthood, particularly motherhood. While the media obsesses about the 'yummy mummy' and the 'slummy mummy', the fact that motherhood is a subject worthy of more complex treatment is overlooked. As Professor Rachel Thomson of the Open University says in her study of modern motherhood: 'Motherhood is a moment of identity change.' Becoming a mother is a huge change in any woman's life – physically, socially and psychologically.

A close friend told me she felt a fraud as a mother. 'I am a 46-year-old full-time working mother in an area where most mothers don't work, I only have one child, when most have two or three, and I was until recently a single mother. I don't have anything in common with these women but we are all mothers.'

An Open University study of first-time mothers in London's poorest borough, Tower Hamlets, examined how culture also intersects with motherhood identity. A Ghanaian mother suggested she would have had a more hallowed status, and more hands-on support, in Ghana where her mother or mother-in-law would have moved in to bath and care for the baby, leaving her to breastfeed 'because you have no experience (bathing) the baby... the only thing you can do is breastfeed'.

The caring role by an experienced relative which she is describing is sometimes occupied, less satisfactorily and only for the upper classes in Britain, by maternity nurses who stay for six to ten weeks with a family at a cost of £700 a week.

Differences in identity were also unearthed when it came to negotiating with the father about responsibility – getting up in the night for example. One mother said her partner was willing, but not until she went back to work herself, and even then she apologised for his likely reluctance to follow-through.

A separate study of transsexual identities, led by Dr Susan Speer of Manchester University – *Constructions of gender in an NHS gender identity clinic* – and looking literally at how gender is constructed, provides a unique insight into how people perceive themselves in relation to others. The study is based on 150 hours of audio recordings of psychiatrist and patient consultations and demonstrates the importance of language in the formation of identity.

One man wanting to change sex was initially confident about his looks, then sought third party affirmation, and – without the overt reassurance of the psychiatrist – finally gave up and decided, poignantly, he needed 'a bag over his head'.

So the issue of identity is multi-faceted and fluid. We often know what we are not, rather than what we are. But there are, as Professor Wetherell points out, strong grounds for policies which emphasise cohesion and respect for diversity within a 'union of many ways of being British' approach.

She argues persuasively that building policy around integration and diversity is about working out ways in which people from different backgrounds can develop an equal, democratic and common life together. 'It is,' she says, 'about creating a "politics of belonging" which balances diversity and commonality... which people find motivating and inspiring.'

Sarah Womack is the Social Affairs Correspondent for the Daily Telegraph. *March 2007*

⇨ Information from the Economic and Social Research Council. Visit www.esrc.ac.uk for more information.

© ESRC

Social class definition

Social Grade: A (approximately 3% of the total population)
These are professional people, very senior managers in business or commerce or top-level civil servants. Retired people, previously social grade A, and their widows.

Social Grade: B (approximately 20% of the total population)
Middle management executives in large organisations, with appropriate qualifications. Principal officers in local government and civil service. Top management or owners of small business concerns, educational and service establishments. Retired people, previously social grade B, and their widows.

Social Grade: C1 (approximately 28% of the total population)
Junior management, owners of small establishments, and all others in non-manual positions. Jobs in this group have very varied responsibilities and educational requirements. Retired people, previously social grade C1, and their widows.

Social Grade: C2 (approximately 21% of the total population)
All skilled manual workers, and those manual workers with responsibility for other people. Retired people, previously social grade C2, with pensions from their job. Widows, if receiving pensions from their late husband's job.

Social Grade: D (approximately 18% of the total population)
All semi-skilled and unskilled manual workers, apprentices and trainees to skilled workers. Retired people, previously grade D, with pensions from their job. Widows, if receiving a pension from their late husband's job.

Social Grade: E (approximately 10% of the total population)
All those entirely dependent on the state long term, through sickness, unemployment, old age or other reasons. Those unemployed for a period exceeding six months. Casual workers and those without a regular income. Only households without a Chief Income Earner will be coded in this group.

⇨ The above information is reprinted with kind permission from the Market Research Society, and is taken from their publication *Occupation Groupings: A Job Dictionary*, 6th edition, 2006. Visit www.mrs.org.uk for more information.

© Market Research Society 2006

Class psychology

The psychology underlying the British class system is what makes it unique, explains Sandra Jovchelovitch

I have been living in Britain for 16 years and during this period have acquired that kind of outsider/insider perspective that anthropologists describe as a mix of estrangement and familiarity. You become part of the place and yet not quite. I have learnt how to enjoy gardening and the best winter puddings in the world, but if there is something I still find intriguing and peculiar about Britain it is the class issue.

Class is central to the collective psyche of this country. Here there is awareness of class, talk about class, jokes about class, and embarrassed glances about class

---

The force of class here is very striking. Certainly stronger than in any other comparable industrialised Western society. Social and cultural psychologists around Europe refer to it jokingly as the 'British hang-up'.

Indeed what makes class in Britain so unique is not so much the reality of the class system, but the psychology that lies beneath it. Class is central to the collective psyche of this country. Here there is awareness of class, talk about class, jokes about class, and embarrassed glances about class.

Accents, manners, intonation, food, impression and expression management are all subtle and pervasive markers that establish from the very beginning who you are and where you belong. Class here is an attitude, something you believe in or you do not, something you argue passionately about, something you feel in your gut and you understand as well as the language you speak.

Quite apart from different positions people occupy in the class system and the different experiences they have in relation to it there is widespread and immediately recognisable shared knowledge about class. Opinions may vary but everyone knows the terms of the debate and what class is about: it has a place at the very core of the collective consciousness of this country.

Such an ingrained way of thinking and behaving around a notion is part of what social psychologists and historians call mentalities. Mentalities are powerful and sticky ideas that run in history, get handed down through generations, are cemented in all kinds of social institutions and ultimately in the behaviour and psychological make-up of individuals. Mentalities are made of beliefs and deep-rooted in behaviour; they are difficult to change and tend to survive long after social structures are gone.

As part of the British mentality, class is resistant to change and difficult to transform because it is deeply entrenched in the way Brits speak – and language is the single most important symbolic system shaping any human community – and in the disciplining of bodies, one of the most powerful psychological mechanisms for socialising the young and reproducing social orders. Every time someone speaks and moves it starts all over again.

Ironically whereas the mentality about class in Britain is unique, its reality is not. The UK situation is not altogether dissimilar from other comparable European countries.

Across the board class still matters, as the strong correlation between educational achievement and family

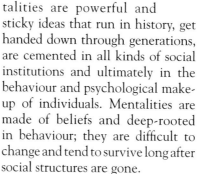
Some activities are still associated with certain social classes

background demonstrates. But there has been tremendous social mobility in the post-war years, which might be slowing down considerably, but not completely.

It would be plainly wrong, and indeed politically undesirable, to state that material distinctions are gone, but the old differences between the upper, middle and working classes have been displaced by more complex scenarios, where diversity of lifestyles and use of income, multiculturalism and new global cultural references complicate distinctions and unsettle the ways in which identities are defined and group affiliations take shape.

The hard consequences of class are real enough for the many people who are at the sharp end of the class system. But these should not overshadow the reality and potential of the many new routes for socialisation and identity that are opening and challenging the social frameworks of class in contemporary Britain.

Today people cross borders and seek identity in ways that were unimagined and indeed almost impossible just a few decades ago. There are new sociabilities in the scene, new ways of organising communities and of establishing social solidarities. This should wake us up to what is new ahead. Britain's old psychology of class needs to catch up.

1 October 2007

⇨ The above information is reprinted with kind permission from the *New Statesman*. Visit www.newstatesman.com for more information.

Middle-class teenagers made 'whipping boys'

Middle-class teenagers are being turned into 'whipping boys' as ministers discriminate against them in favour of students from poor homes, teachers warned.

Education is being 'dumbed down' as universities turn their attention towards easy subjects like surfing studies, beauty therapy and knitwear to attract more working-class students, it is claimed.

In a fierce attack, the Professional Association of Teachers called for the Government to halt its drive towards so-called 'social engineering'.

The comments come amid controversy over policies designed to increase the number of university students from state schools and deprived backgrounds.

Ministers want to see half of all school-leavers studying beyond the age of 18 and have given dons tough targets to attract 'hard to reach' students.

But Peter Morris, chairman of the PAT in Wales, accused ministers of 'creating barriers in education based on social class'.

Addressing the union's annual conference in Harrogate, he said: 'I am angry because this Government has interfered with my children and their children's chances of getting a good education in this country.

'They have changed the ways that examinations are assessed, and clearly this has had a "dumbing down" effect

By Graeme Paton, Education Correspondent

on the academic standards, in order to get more pupils to achieve.'

Under new rules, teenagers applying for university will be asked to say whether their parents have degrees in an attempt to attract more students from poor homes. But Mr Morris insisted it amounted to discrimination against middle-class pupils.

'This political interfering with university applications clearly is designed to reduce the chances of hard-working applicants getting places,' he said.

'How can any academic institution make a selection of candidates for university courses based on the perceived social class of the parents?

'The middle classes are becoming the new whipping boys for "New Labour".'

Criticising the Government's education record, Mr Morris, a retired teacher from Swansea, said exams had gone from being academically rigorous to posing 'woolly, touchy-feely' questions with little intellectual merit to act as a leg-up to the working classes.

Courses such as physics, chemistry and maths have been replaced with 'non-academic' degrees such as 'surfing, beauty therapy, knitwear, circus skills, pig enterprise management, death studies, air guitar, David Beckham studies and wine studies', he said.

The comments come just days after universities were accused of cashing in on soft courses by plugging degrees in subjects such as complementary medicine.

It was disclosed that applications for complementary medicine are up more than 31 per cent this year, while there has been a 19 per cent fall in applications to study anatomy, physiology and pathology.

Speaking at the PAT conference, Nardia Foster, a psychology teacher

from Enfield, north London, said that Labour had created a more 'fractured, divided, selfish society'.

'There is a lack of consistency, stability, moral integrity and fairness in our society,' she said.

Teenagers applying for university will be asked to say whether their parents have degrees

'To dumb down declares to the whole world "British children are stupid".'

Geraldine Everett, PAT chairman, said universities should not set 'quotas' for admissions.

'It is wrong to manufacture reasons to put one group forward ahead of another,' she said.

'It is an invasion of privacy to take account of parental background. Places should go on merit – not your parents' education.'

Last month it emerged that leading institutions were actually taking fewer students from deprived areas – despite the Government's drive to redress their middle-class bias.

Teenagers from wealthier families and private schools increased their hold on places at half of the 20 most sought-after universities, according to official figures.

A spokesman for the newly-formed Department for Children, Schools and Families said: 'We are ensuring every child has the best possible start in life and the opportunity to succeed – nobody can argue with that.

'New ways of raising standards in schools, such as progression and personalisation, will ensure that all pupils get the education they deserve to reach their full potential. And it is only right that we are also ensuring the opportunity of higher education is accessible to everyone who desires it.'
1 August 2007

Chavs and chav nots

Is mockery of the chav just class-based snobbery?

What started out as a genuine concern within working class communities about the rise in the number and severity of instances of anti-social behaviour being carried out by young people on our estates, has now been hijacked by the right-wing media and elevated into a cultural witch-hunt of working-class youth.

No matter that the vast majority of working-class kids, despite being amongst the poorest in the western world, are not engaged in acts of violence and vandalism. All are now branded 'chavs' and 'hoodies' and are alternately portrayed as either figures of fun or the new enemy within.

And yet little is said about the fighting, assaults and vandalism in the towns of Rock and Daymer Bay in Cornwall, where every year up to 700 public school pupils take part in all-night beach parties, using local hedgerows and fences to build bonfires. By the end of the summer holidays last year, 103 crimes had been recorded on Daymer and Polzeath beaches, and eight arrests had been made, prompting local residents to hire private security guards to protect them.

So it was refreshing to read the views of Matthew Holehouse, a Year 12 grammar school pupil and *Times Educational Supplement* columnist, who identifies the anti-chav phenomenon for exactly what it is: 'class-based snobbery'.

Don't mock the chav
It's not big or clever to make fun of disadvantaged teenagers, it's just plain old class-based snobbery, writes Matthew Holehouse.
Chavs! They're everywhere! High streets and shopping centres are being swamped. Sporting Burberry caps, tracksuits, shaven heads and white trainers, smoking, spitting and looking shifty, hordes of youths coalesce outside McDonald's and in parks across the country to drink cheap cider and listen to Eminem. No town, it seems, is safe from the chavalanche.

And how we laugh at them. Last Christmas you could buy chav joke books, which were essentially rehashed Irish and dumb blondes gags. *Little Britain*'s Vicky Pollard has been hailed as a work of genius. Wayne Rooney won fame for brilliant football, and sustains it for having a chav name and a leopard-print chav girlfriend.

More sinisterly, websites have sprung up, inviting visitors to send in pictures of the local 'chav scum' and buy 'hilarious' anti-chav wristbands. They've become synonymous, rather unjustly, with muggings, vandalism and yobbery. When Tony Blair talks about a 'culture of respect' in Britain, and newspapers demand action against the 'gangs of feral youths', we all know whom they mean. Chav-bashing is a national hobby, and sadly, it's now OK for us to loathe our contemporaries.

Hang on a second. Being a chav, I think, stems from more than simple choice. John Prescott might claim that 'we're all middle class now', but chavs are essentially working-class white kids who dare to appear in public. They don't aspire to be accountants and they don't live in suburbia. They have the temerity to buy fake designer labels, not because they can't tell the difference from the genuine article, but because they don't have hundreds of pounds spare to buy it. One newspaper article smugly referred to them as a 'peasant underclass'. In a way they're probably more right than they intended.

Mocking the way disadvantaged teenagers live isn't biting social satire, so much as old-fashioned, class-based snobbery. It's not the association with anti-social behaviour that makes them a legitimate target for public ridicule, but their social faux pas. Chavs aren't criminal, just frightful. In a sense the way they express themselves is immaterial; it's just the fact that they're, well, there. Remember the Victorian idea of the 'undeserving poor'? They're alive and well and shopping at JJB Sports.

I recently stayed in a private boarding school for a schools' seminar. On the dorm corridors they had framed pictures of their chav-themed Christmas disco, with tall, rosy-cheeked, foppish Year 9s in Nike tracksuits and gold chains, pulling unconvincing rapper poses. It was an admirable effort: sovereign rings must be quite hard to come by in rural Shropshire. If you're 14 and missing the world outside of school it would, I suppose, have been fun.

It's not big or clever to make fun of disadvantaged teenagers

---

But swapping blazer and jeans for tracksuit and bling is basically class tourism; privileged kids having a good time by pretending to be people living on sink estates who, chances are, they've never even met. It's a *Black and White Minstrel Show* for our generation (only with worse dancing). If schools are meant to instil some sense of equality and respect, rather than confirming schoolboy prejudices about people from other backgrounds, then this sort of thing has to go. Teachers ought to play a part in discouraging such hostility. Otherwise, we're just asking to have our phones nicked. Innit.

⇨ The introduction to this article is reproduced with kind permission from the Independent Working Class Association. The article 'Don't mock the chav' is copyright to Matthew Holehouse, and originally appeared in the Times Educational Supplement.
© IWCA / Matthew Holehouse

A child's-eye view of social difference

Children's perceptions of social difference – extract from a report by the Joseph Rowntree Foundation

Introduction: poor, rich, 'chavs' and 'posh'

This article considers how the children viewed themselves in relation to others from different backgrounds.

Social difference on socio-economic grounds was keenly perceived and described in terms of 'chavs' and 'posh' children

They did not identify themselves as poor or affluent. Indeed, both the estate children and the private schoolchildren used these terms to' distinguish 'other' people from themselves. As this article considers how children use 'poverty' as a term to identify others, we begin by locating these observations in other research that highlights the stigmatising potential of the 'poverty' label. We then explore how children perceive themselves in relation to poverty and affluence, before considering how they talked about social differences. Social difference on socio-economic grounds was keenly perceived and described in terms of 'chavs' and 'posh' children – associated with lower and higher socio-economic circumstances respectively. The article concludes by considering the implications of these observations for children and policy.

Children, poverty and stigma

Tess Ridge (2002) found that poverty had a profound impact on every aspect of the lives of children and young people, from the material through to the social and emotional. Poverty is, as Ridge demonstrated, a stigmatised social position. It carries with it the notion that poorer people have 'less'

JOSEPH ROWNTREE FOUNDATION

and do 'worse'. Thus, in the words of one 16-year-old:
I don't think anybody's ever going to tell you that they're in poverty. (Quoted in Willow, 2001, p. 5)

Ridge also argued that:
… the labels that society attaches to poor children will have a profound impact on how children see themselves and on how other children see them. (Ridge, 2002, p. 144)

Children as members of society are also responsible for labelling and stereotyping each other. We need to explore how children from different socio-economic circumstances perceive themselves and each other, in order to contribute towards a fuller understanding of different childhood identities and experiences.

Being 'normal' ('not being different')

The children were asked to consider pictures of different children engaged in various activities and to talk about where they saw them belonging when placed in a line from rich through to poor. This promoted a discussion about their own circumstances. Neither the estate children nor the private schoolchildren defined or talked about themselves as either poor or rich. They were all eager to be seen as 'average' along a continuum of poverty through to affluence:
G: I've got one dog and I had a cat when I had the dog, now I've still got that cat and I've got two more kittens.
LS: Really?
G: Yes and I'm not rich and I'm not poor. I'm nearly in the middle.
(Older estate girl)

The children's desire to avoid differentiating themselves from others was reflected in how they presented their circumstances. The estate children tended to 'talk up' what they owned; as one estate boy said, 'I've got all the stuff I want'. The private schoolchildren sometimes 'talked down' their material possessions and, particularly, played down their relative economic status:
We live in a nice big house with a drive, but I wouldn't say I was more highly put than anybody else really. We are moving into a big house with a drive, but I wouldn't really be like that to anybody else. There are some children who get like absolutely everything they ask for, but like I don't get everything I ask for. (Older private schoolgirl)

It is hardly surprising that children living in relative poverty do not wish to identify with the terms 'poor' or 'poverty', not least because being poor is such a stigmatised position. Furthermore, some of these children may have felt that they had to 'save face' within a group setting. Similarly, some affluent children did not want to be considered 'spoilt' or as having things that other children might go without. Indeed, when the private schoolchildren saw the estate children's list of important things, some of them remarked that they felt 'shallow' by comparison.

The 'otherness' of poverty and affluence

The fact that the children distanced themselves from notions of poverty and affluence reflected the fact that they defined poverty and wealth in extreme terms and to signify social 'otherness'.

This was demonstrated, for example, during the exercise in which the estate children were asked to order pictures of different children along a rich-poor continuum. The children identified only one as belonging in the 'poor' group – a black girl with dreadlocks wearing a white dress. When asked why, the children explained that she was poor because she came from Africa.

G: *Because it's Africa. They can't afford proper clothes. And these [other pictures of children] are right up here because they've got Burberry tops on and they've got Bench, they've got make-up, clothes.*
(Older estate girl)

Both the estate children and the private schoolchildren then talked about poverty, to begin with, in relation to the absolute definition of poverty. They referred to people who were homeless and hungry. During role-play sessions with the estate children, poor people were always represented as beggars living on the streets and desperate for food and money. There were some subtle differences in how the estate children and the private schoolchildren discussed poverty. The private schoolchildren, for example, acknowledged the relative nature of poverty and were aware that people who 'hadn't got as much stuff as us' were poorer. They therefore recognised that they could be considered 'better off' because they had more material possessions than others. The private schoolchildren also identified that those living on council estates would not have much money and, as such, would have less choice about where they lived.

The estate children, on the other hand, believed that several things contributed to being poor. For example, having a low-paid or in their terms 'unsuccessful' job meant that they might have difficulties in being able to pay for or retain a house. In the estate children's eyes, being poor also made a person less selfish than being rich:

They would have to think about other people, even though they're starving on the streets, they could be thinking about their family and their friends who have died and stuff. They wouldn't just be thinking about themselves and how hungry they are. Because they're thinking about how to help other people who've lost their jobs.
(Older estate girl)

They also demonstrated a keen sense of social justice with regards to helping 'poor people', who were generally viewed with sympathy:
Give them food and give them some more money so that they can buy themselves a house and they can buy some food.
(Younger estate boy)

Wealth or affluence was also generally viewed in extreme terms by both the estate children and the private schoolchildren. Being rich meant having larger material possessions and more of them. Typical comments were that the rich owned very large houses and lots of cars. Their houses would have numerous bathrooms, 'golden baths' and spacious rooms. They would have an enormous garden – usually complemented with a swimming pool, a conservatory and invariably a huge trampoline. However, the estate children perceived people who owned certain things to be wealthier than others. For example, rich people owned horses and children who wore 'nice', 'clean' or designer clothes were also perceived to be richer than others.

Socio-economic difference: being 'chavs' and being 'posh'

While poverty and wealth were generally associated with extreme one-dimensional caricatures, the children presented a far richer and in-depth discussion on social difference through their frequent references to 'chavs' and 'posh people'.

The children defined themselves in terms of what they were not rather than what they were. For example, the private schoolchildren spoke about 'chavs' as being at one end of a spectrum and 'rich' as being at the other end, and they placed themselves somewhere in the middle of that continuum. The private schoolchildren opined that 'chavs' – distinguishable because of their outfits of tracksuits, hoods and baseball caps

– were not necessarily poor, but were 'common' and behaved badly.
B1: *Chavs just are like the people who mess around.*
B2: *Common people are chavs.*
B3: *Poor people are just people who don't have any money and common people are like they hate like people who like going to [private] schools like [ours] and they'll like beat you up.*
B2: *And if you go to like a school where you have to pay a lot, saying like you're really rich.*
(Older private schoolboys)

Some children described having been picked on by 'chavs' because they went to a private school and had a highly identifiable uniform. They also highlighted how their uniforms marked them out as being 'posh' or 'snobs' when they considered themselves not to be. They believed that they were often misjudged and mislabelled.

'Chav' was used specifically by the private schoolchildren to refer to children who lived on estates and who had parents who were unemployed, with poor parenting skills. When we explored these perceptions further, by asking how life might be different for children living on council estates, the private schoolchildren began by blaming the children's parents for chavs' bad behaviour.
B1: *Their parents would be a bad example, they would smoke in front of them and they would swear and drink, you know.*
B2: *The parents wouldn't care about them, would they? They wouldn't care what they do and just let them go off.*
(Older private schoolboys)

This attitude is also evident in the following discussion between two private schoolgirls when they were also asked how life might be different for children living on a council estate. Their views resonate with current research undertaken by MORI on public attitudes towards poverty (Thompson and Castell, 2006):
G1: *I suppose kids would have it rough because they wouldn't have as much money. But they still might have as much love, like the families might be there because they can't get a good enough job, because their parents haven't had the money to give them an education or they were brought up wrong, they weren't brought up to be bright. So they might*

love their children very much but they can't give them what they need.

G2: It's tough on the parents. If they didn't have a good job they should have worked extra jobs to get the money.

G1: I know, they might try but they still wouldn't have as much money would they?

G2: Yes but they could have had more.

G1: It is like saying because we aren't millionaires we should work ten other jobs just to get to be a millionaire.

G2: No. What I am saying is they don't have enough money to give to the children the extra schooling to give them more opportunities or help them on the way to university.

(Older private schoolgirls)

The above quote demonstrates a common theme among the private schoolchildren when they discussed those living on council estates. Two views were generally put forward on the topic. One view would be more sympathetic, acknowledging the 'tough' job that parents have in bringing up children in poorer economic circumstances. The other view tended to blame parents for their poor parenting skills or their inability to get enough work to enable them to 'lift' children out of poverty. What is also apparent from this discussion is the girls' belief that poorer children do not have the opportunities that they have to get a decent education.

The estate children used an alternative way of distinguishing themselves from others. For example, they referred frequently to people with drug and alcohol problems who lived on their estate, describing them as 'druggies' and 'smack heads'. The children perceived these people to be a major source of problems on the estate and they were unsympathetic, disparaging and critical about them. In this sense, the estate children's 'starting point' for their social continuum was different to that of the private schoolchildren. Whereas the private schoolchildren distinguished themselves from 'chavs' and rich people, the estate children suggested a continuum that ranged from 'druggies' through to posh people.

Rather than the term 'chav', the estate children tended to talk about 'scallys' (short for scallywags) and 'gangsters'. Gangsters and scallys were described in the same way as the private schoolchildren described 'chavs' – in terms of both dress codes and bad behaviour – except the estate children talked about scallys as a feature of local life, sometimes referring to and discussing alleged 'scallys' by name. The girls tended to be more critical about scallys than the boys, whose discussions belied some sense of disguised admiration.

'Chav' was used specifically by the private schoolchildren to refer to children who lived on estates and who had parents who were unemployed, with poor parenting skills

---

Although some of the private schoolchildren felt that 'chavs' were not necessarily poor, they nevertheless associated 'chavs' with disadvantaged backgrounds and public housing. Some of the estate children similarly felt that being a 'scally' did not necessarily equate with poverty, though one of the older girls commented that 'you could be [rich and a scally] but they'd only call you a scally if you're poor'. This indicates that these children were also aware of the negative labels – generally associated with bad behaviour – that can be attached to less well-off children.

The estate children were reproachful about people they perceived as being rich. They used role play to express their opinions about rich people being spiteful, mean and greedy. Being rich also meant being 'posh' and 'snobby'. It meant being different – talking differently, living in a different type of house and wearing a different style of clothes.

During later discussions, the estate children believed that richer children would have difficulty in making and keeping friends. They felt that having money meant that they would be likely to 'show off' and that jealousy would mean that some children would shun them while others would bully them. The estate children also felt that private schoolchildren would have little fun in their lives because their parents would be paying for them to get a 'good' education and the emphasis therefore would be on working hard:

B1: They've got the money but they don't have the fun.

B2: We have the fun without money and they have the money without the fun.

B3: They stay in too much doing home-work and they don't make hardly any friends. That's why people pick on them.

(Older estate boys)

These assumptions made by the estate children about the private schoolchildren's lives were both confirmed and challenged during the fieldwork. First, some of the private schoolchildren confirmed that the amount and extent of the work they needed to do at private school was demanding. However, they also knew that it was a requirement in their lives and ostensibly 'for their own good'. They had to do their 'prep' or

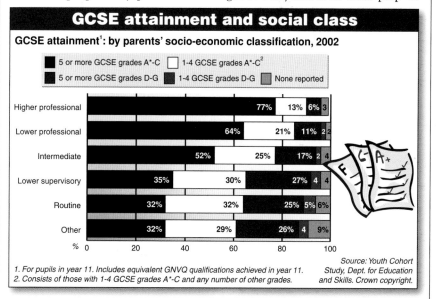

GCSE attainment and social class

GCSE attainment[1]: by parents' socio-economic classification, 2002

| | 5 or more GCSE grades A*-C | 1-4 GCSE grades A*-C[2] |
| | 5 or more GCSE grades D-G | 1-4 GCSE grades D-G | None reported |

	5 or more A*-C	1-4 A*-C	5 or more D-G	1-4 D-G	None
Higher professional	77%	13%	6%	3	
Lower professional	64%	21%	11%	2	2
Intermediate	52%	25%	17%	2	4
Lower supervisory	35%	30%	27%	4	4
Routine	32%	32%	25%	5%	6%
Other	32%	29%	26%	4	9%

% 0   20   40   60   80   100

1. For pupils in year 11. Includes equivalent GNVQ qualifications achieved in year 11.
2. Consists of those with 1-4 GCSE grades A*-C and any number of other grades.

Source: Youth Cohort Study, Dept. for Education and Skills. Crown copyright.

homework before they could consider doing any other activity. Their particular childhood culture was focused on learning and, particularly, learning in order to get on and do well in the future. However, they argued that they did have friends but we found that they did not always see them as often as they wanted to because of the amount of homework they had to do. They also did not share a community or neighbourhood where they could play out with friends in the same way as the estate children did.

Private schoolchildren also confirmed that they had been picked on by 'chavs' because they were different and to some extent because they were perceived to have money. Indeed the older private schoolboys talked about what happened to them when they went to stay in a residential adventure setting, which accepted both state and private schools:

B1: *There was like this adventure place where you go to stay for a week and there was these three chavs and they just kept on like messing around with our school and hurting people in our school and that ...*
B2: *... they took my wallet and I had £20 in it.*
B1: *I know. One of them nicked my watch and he was like throwing it at, because they're taller than us, they were throwing it around and I was trying to jump and catch it but I couldn't.*
(Older private schoolboys)

The estate children's assumptions that the private schoolchildren would not have any fun were partly borne out by the private schoolchildren's extra emphasis on learning and achieving. However, the private schoolchildren recognised that this educational focus gave them advantages and opportunities for the future that they felt estate children would not have.

Social difference, identity and diversity

The children living in relative poverty did not perceive themselves to be poor. Arguably, this could relate to one or a number of factors. As mentioned previously, poverty is a socially stigmatised position and the children were aware of this. Parents may also protect their children from the immediate manifestations of poverty. Indeed,

a few parents mentioned their strategies for aiding their financial situation and protecting their children by buying cheaper items of school uniform so the children were not identified as different in this respect. The children's parents may also have transmitted to their children that there were people who were 'worse off' than them. Poverty and affluence in today's society are, after all, relative concepts. This does not mean, however, that we should understate the impact of poverty – especially as the research does not look at the longer-term or lifelong effect of poverty – but it does carry implications for researching relative poverty from children's perspectives.

Allison James (1993) has argued that there is no single childhood culture. Children are a heterogeneous group whose only commonality is that they are children. She has also highlighted the role of stereotyping in children's culture and demonstrated how being different has had a profound impact on the lives of children. This article suggests that, while the children share some elements in their world views – namely their desire to avoid standing out – their socio-economic backgrounds have a strong impact on their understanding of who they are and who they are not.

This research suggests that the children, from as young as eight years of age, perceive social divisions on socio-economic grounds. Although the children – when invited to reflect on these divisions – could appreciate that individuals were not necessarily responsible for their circumstances, and could demonstrate non-judgemental attitudes and a sense of social justice, this was not their dominant language. Instead, when the estate children discussed 'rich/posh' people, and the private schoolchildren discussed 'chavs', all of them presented a markedly antagonistic attitude towards social difference. By saying that 'chavs' misbehave, live in families that do not care about them and go to 'rough' schools, the private schoolchildren are effectively saying that this is not us and we do not belong to them. Similarly, by saying that 'posh' children are snobby, have no friends or fun, the estate children are also

stressing that they do not belong to that group or way of life.

The children, then, were aware of how they could be perceived in wider society. Their socio-economic backgrounds help to constitute their understanding of their own sense of belonging and identity. The children's antagonistic attitude towards social difference on these grounds has implications for their lives now and in the future – particularly for the self-esteem and life chances of those from poorer backgrounds. If children are to grow up in a society that truly respects diversity, we need to address some of the ways that they view socio-economic differences. Critically reflecting on these issues as part of a school's citizenship education curriculum may be one way of doing so. *From the report* A child's-eye view of social difference *by Liz Sutton, Noel Smith, Chris Dearden and Sue Middleton. Published in September 2007 by the Joseph Rowntree Foundation.*

⇨ The above information is reprinted with kind permission from the Joseph Rowntree Foundation. Visit www.jrf.org.uk for more information.
© *Joseph Rowntree Foundation*

Health and social class

Information from Patient Plus

Background

There has always been an association between health and social class and despite the welfare state and the improvement in health in all sections of societies over the years this discrepancy remains. It applies to all aspects of health including expectation of life, infant and maternal mortality and general level of health. Whilst the failure to close the social gap is a disgrace to some, others would claim that so long as these parameters are improving in all levels of society there is no cause for concern. Despite nearly 60 years of the National Health Service, there remain marked differences in all parameters of health across the social classes, there is significant geographical variation and women, on average, live 5 years longer than men.

Social class is a complex issue that may involve status, wealth, culture, background and employment. The relationship between class and ill health is not simple. There are a number of different influences on health, some of which include social class. In 1943 Sigerist, following the line of Virchow, wrote, 'The task of medicine is to promote health, to prevent disease, to treat the sick when prevention is broken down and to rehabilitate the people after they have been cured. These are highly social functions and we must look at medicine as basically a social science.'

The greatest influences on the improvement in health with longer expectancy of life, lower infant mortality, etc., have been not so much medical discoveries as improved social conditions.

History

In 1572 an Elizabethan Act made provision for the punishment of sturdy beggars and the relief of the impotent poor. A similar law followed in Scotland in 1574. In England an Act of 1601 made provision for 'setting the poor on work'. This did not generally include accommodation, but in 1631 a workhouse was established in Abingdon and in 1697 the Bristol Workhouse was established by private Act of Parliament. Scotland had 'houses of correction' established in the burghs, by an Act of 1672. Some people regarded all this as too liberal and in 1834 Malthus argued that the population was increasing beyond the ability of the country to feed it. The Poor Law was seen as an encouragement to illegitimacy, and this would lead in turn to mass starvation.

Social class is a complex issue that may involve status, wealth, culture, background and employment. The relationship between class and ill health is not simple

---

Edwin Chadwick published his 'General Report on the Sanitary conditions of the Labouring Population of Great Britain' in 1842. This showed that the average age at death in Liverpool at that time was 35 for gentry and professionals but only 15 for labourers, mechanics and servants. In 1901 Seebohm Rowntree was able not only to trace in detail the sanitary defects of areas of York but he was able to compare the general mortality rates, infant mortality rates and heights and weights of children of different ages in three areas of York, distinguished according to the proportions living below his poverty line, and compared with the servant keeping classes. The Rowntree family founded the famous chocolate company. They were, and still are, a Quaker family with a great social conscience as shown through the Joseph Rowntree Foundation and Trust.

The National Health Service

A government document in 1944 stated: 'One of the fundamental principles of the National Health Service is to divorce the care of health from questions of personal means or other factors irrelevant to it.'

Aneurin Bevan convinced the Treasury to fund the incredibly expensive package of the NHS in 1948, at a time of post-war austerity and massive nationalisation by the Labour government with the argument that a national health service, free at the point of access, would so improve the health of the nation that the percentage of GDP spent on health would diminish. He was succeeded by Enoch Powell as

Class and mortality in 1971

The following table shows death rates by sex and social (occupational) class in those aged 15 to 64 years in rates per 1000 population. It relates to England and Wales 1971 and males refers to all males but females refers to married women only and classifies them by their husband's social class.

Social (Occupational) Class	Males	Females	Ratio M/F
I (Professional)	3.98	2.15	1.85
II (Intermediate)	5.54	2.85	1.94
IIIn (Skilled non-manual)	5.80	2.76	1.96
IIIm (Skilled manual)	6.08	3.41	1.78
IV (Partly Skilled)	7.96	4.27	1.87
V (Unskilled)	9.88	5.31	1.86
Ratio V / I	2.5	2.5	

Source: Tudor Hart J, 'The inverse care law'. Lancet 27 February 1971. Taken from the document 'Health and Social Class', from Patient Plus.

Minister of Health after a general election. He found that there is no limit to the amount of money that could be spent on a national health service. It is a bottomless pit.

Causes of health inequalities

The relationship between social class and what are now called health inequalities is clear from simple observation. They affect not just adults but children too. The reason why they occur merits discussion.

⇨ The question of *post hoc ergo propter hoc* (chicken or the egg) asks if it is the low social class that has led to the poor health or if poor health has led to a deterioration of social status. Studies of patients with schizophrenia showed that they tend to belong to the lower social classes but this is much less marked for their fathers and this suggests that it is the disease that has caused the low social class rather than the low social class that predisposes to the disease. However, most chronic diseases tend to present rather later in life, well into adulthood and after careers have been decided and the association with social class is not found. Hence, even looking at the question from the opposite direction and suggesting that the healthy will tend to rise through the social classes does not seem feasible.

⇨ The material explanation blames poverty, poor housing conditions, lack of resources in health and educational provision as well as higher risk occupations for the poor health of the lower social classes. Poverty is demonstrably bad for health. Life expectancy is low in poorer, less developed countries, but the diseases that afflict the developed world tend to be related to obesity and tobacco and injudicious consumption of alcohol. Within the wealthy nations we find that they are most prevalent in their poorest regions and the lower social classes.

⇨ The cultural explanation suggests that the lower social classes prefer less healthy lifestyles, eat more fatty foods, smoke more and exercise less than the middle and upper classes. They have less

money to spend on a healthy diet although this is probably rather less important than a lack of knowledge of what is a healthy diet. People who have been on their feet all day in shops or factories are less likely than office workers to seek activity in the evening although their daily work has not been adequate to exercise the cardio-respiratory system. Despite the phrase as drunk as a lord, the association between binge drinking and social class has been readily noted and Frederick Engels wrote that 'Drink is the bane of the working classes.' Oscar Wilde inverted this to 'Work is the bane of the drinking classes.' Before the first report on *Smoking and Health* by the Royal College of Physicians there was little difference in the incidence of smoking between social classes. Now there is a distinct gradation across social classes. It may seem reasonable to suggest that when money is short that the first place for economies should be in the consumption of alcohol and tobacco but surveys have shown that in times of economic recession, there is no decline in demand. There is evidence that risk behaviours are unevenly distributed between the social classes and that this contributes

to the health gradient. Health is also better in those of higher intelligence as measured by IQ but this does not account for all of the disparity.

⇨ Social capital is a term used for how connected people are to their communities through work, family, membership of clubs, faith groups, political and social organisations. This has also been shown to have an impact on health. During the 1950s and 60s a study of the Italian-American community of Roseto, Pennsylvania, where heart attacks were 50% less frequent than surrounding communities, explained these differences by the greater social cohesion of this group. This concept has been confirmed by other workers. The idea that social isolation is bad for health is also supported by self-report studies that show housewives, the unemployed and the retired as reporting significantly poorer health than those who are employed.

⇨ The above information is an extract from an article published by Patient Plus and is reprinted with permission. Visit www.patient.co.uk for more information.

© EMIS 2008, *as distributed on www. patient.co.uk*

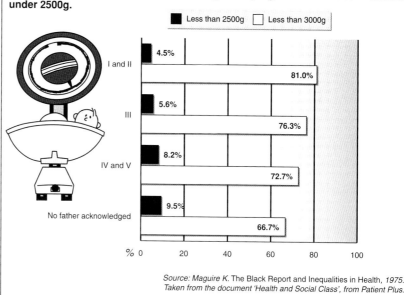

Class and birth weight in 1975

The following graph shows birth weights of babies by father's social class and those with no father acknowledged, from Chamberlain 1975. It shows how going through the social classes down to where no father was acknowledged there was a progressive decline in babies over 3000g and a progressive increase in babies under 2500g.

■ Less than 2500g □ Less than 3000g

I and II: 4.5% / 81.0%
III: 5.6% / 76.3%
IV and V: 8.2% / 72.7%
No father acknowledged: 9.5% / 66.7%

% 0   20   40   60   80   100

Source: Maguire K. The Black Report and Inequalities in Health, 1975. Taken from the document 'Health and Social Class', from Patient Plus.

Life expectancy and social class

Variations persist in life expectancy by social class – 2002-2005 data released

The variations in life expectancy among social classes which have been found in previous studies persist, according to new figures issued today by the Office for National Statistics. The new data, derived from the ONS Longitudinal Study, cover the period 2002-05 for the first time.

national STATiSTiCS

In the period 2002-05 males in the professional class had a life expectancy at birth of 80.0, compared with 72.7 years for those in the manual unskilled class

While life expectancy has risen for all social classes over the last 30 years, people in professional occupations (Social Class I) have the longest expectation of life, followed by managerial and technical occupations (Social Class II), and so on. People in unskilled manual occupations (Social Class V) have the shortest expectation of life.

In the period 2002-05:

⇨ Males in the professional class had a life expectancy at birth of 80.0, compared with 72.7 years for those in the manual unskilled class.

⇨ Females in the professional class had a life expectancy at birth of 85.1 years compared with 78.1 years for the unskilled manual class.

⇨ Unskilled men (Social Class V) aged 65 could expect to live a further 14.1 years, fractionally above the expectation of life professional men would have had in 1972-76 (14.0 years).

⇨ Unskilled women aged 65 had an expectation of life of 17.7 years, less than professional women in 1972-76 (19.1 years).

Taking the period of analysis as a whole, from 1972-76 to 2002-05:

⇨ Both males and females classified to non-manual occupations had a greater increase in life expectancy at birth and at age 65 than those classified to manual occupations.

⇨ For men, there was an increase in life expectancy at birth of 8.0 years for those classified to non-manual occupations compared with 6.8 years for those classified as manual.

⇨ For women, these figures were 5.2 years and 4.8 years respectively.

By contrast, between 1997-2001 and 2002-05:

⇨ Life expectancy for males at birth and at age 65 increased more for manual than non-manual groups.

⇨ For women, estimates of life expectancy increased by a similar amount for those classified to non-manual and manual occupations.

Care should be taken in interpreting the figures. Some degree of variation is to be expected as a result of sampling and the results for the latest period, while interesting, are not conclusive evidence of an underlying change in the pattern of inequalities.

24 October 2007

⇨ The above information is reprinted with kind permission from the Office for National Statistics. Visit www.statistics.gov.uk for more information.

© *Crown copyright*

A question of class – and tomatoes

'Boy meets girl. Boy and girl like each other. Boy and girl go out together. Boy and girl become an item. Boy gets tired of girl. Boy drops girl. There, I've dragged it out for 29 words.' By Peter Wilby

Boy meets girl. Boy and girl like each other. Boy and girl go out together. Boy and girl become an item. Boy gets tired of girl. Boy drops girl. There, I've dragged it out for 29 words. But I need another 1,171 to fill this column. If I were a red-top editor, I'd need to fill at least eight pages and even editors of posh papers want double-page spreads.

Prince William and Kate Middleton, according to the *Sun*, which broke the story of the split, had 'reached an amicable agreement'. They hadn't shouted or thrown things or accused each other of infidelity. Spoilsports.

An issue was, therefore, needed, preferably one that could run for a day or two – until Des Browne resigned or somebody went berserk with a gun on an American campus – spawning features and column leads. The British press can't allow things just to happen. Someone must be to blame. *The Times* boringly insisted, over two successive days, that the issue was that young men don't like early marriage, the average age for their weddings now being 32. That sounds as if it might be Gordon Brown's fault – most things are at the moment – but it's hard to prove and *The Times* didn't try.

The other papers had a better issue, complete with a guilty party. Kate Middleton's mother, Carole, was to blame and she faced full-scale character assassination for being 'brassy and forward' (*News of the World*), 'a ferocious social climber' (*Mail on Sunday*) and, above all, too 'common' (all the papers). The press loves nothing better than to blow the dust off Nancy Mitford, get on the phone to Peter York and instruct us on the nuances of the English class system. All of a sudden, we were back in the 1950s, perhaps even the 1920s, in a world of 'fast and loose sets', of

young men 'dallying' with 'society beauties', of girls called Isabella Anstruther-Gough-Calthorpe and Lady Rosanagh Innes-Ker, and of people worrying about whether to say 'lavatory' or 'toilet'.

Carole Middleton is a former flight attendant who, with her husband, now runs a mail-order company called Party Pieces. She had, the Sunday papers advised us, chewed gum throughout William's graduation ceremony at Sandhurst. Worse, when introduced to the Queen, she said 'pleased to meet you' and 'pardon'. These social gaffes were committed at Sandhurst according to some papers, or at the St Andrews University graduation according to others.

Clarence House tells me that the Queen and Mrs Middleton met on neither occasion (and, indeed, have never met at all), that the Queen has never inquired about what Mrs Middleton calls the, er, you know, thingamijiggy, and she wouldn't care anyway. To my mind, that's a better story, which the press missed. Wasn't the Queen receiving intelligence reports? Did she read them? If not, why not? For heaven's sake, this is the royal succession at stake and, for all we know, Mrs Middleton is a Muslim hate preacher in disguise. The *Daily Mail* should have pulled its socks up and got 10 unanswered questions together.

Instead, the class bandwagon rolled on. Just in case their readers' daughters ever get close to marrying a prince, the press was replete with helpful advice. Even the *Independent* – which had initially followed its custom of ignoring the British royals by running two pages about the Spanish royals – offered 'a bluffer's guide to being posh'. In the *Daily Mail*, AN Wilson explained that we should say 'writing paper', not 'notepaper', 'glasses', not

'spectacles', 'napkin', not 'serviette'. You should say 'lunch' or 'dinner', not 'meal', the *Spectator*'s Mary Killen told this paper's John Harris, and you should never have a tomato in the house (don't ask). The *Telegraph* had a quiz on which I scored so well that it told me, 'you probably have a coat of arms'. But then I'm such a social climber that I feign deafness so I can practise shouting 'what?', which, as we aspirants know, is what you should say instead of 'pardon'. And I haven't even got daughters.

There was, to be sure, more than a hint of irony in these pieces. But by the time the story had crossed to the west coast of America, irony had pretty well disappeared. 'The Middleton affair has reminded Britain ... that it has not yet achieved its aspiration of a classless society,' growled the *Los Angeles Times*.

As for the Middletons, 'close sources' revealed to the *London Evening Standard* last Tuesday that they were 'concerned'. A day later, their condition, as they say in the hospital bulletins, had deteriorated. 'Carole is at breaking point,' the *Sun* was informed by 'a close friend'. So the woman is hysterical, as well as vulgar.

All ended happily, therefore. Newspaper readers had binged on stories about snobbery, a pushy woman had been put firmly in her place, and journalists could move on to speculating about William's next love, installing Isabella Anstruther-etc. as favourite on no better evidence other than that the papers happen to have nice pictures of her legs.

Then came the tale of another young man, Cho Seung-hui. And we could ignore the slaughter in Iraq for a few more days.

23 April 2007

Forget class, it's postcodes that count

Research shows we're no longer identified by social standing but where we live

Britain is a nation defined by its postcodes. Big business is increasingly using address details to label people according to their jobs, family make-up, spending, holiday preferences – even life expectancy.

New research suggests specialist firms can produce 'frighteningly accurate' profiles using a vast database built up from loyalty cards, census details, credit card spending and loan applications. Crime statistics, house prices, school results, insurance claims and even hospital admissions are also fed into the equation.

One of the main firms involved, financial services company Experian, has identified 61 specific types of people, or British tribes, using a system called MOSAIC. The company claims it can produce an accurate profile of a person based on their postcode, which is likely to cover as few as 14 houses in a street.

This will show whether we drive a Lada or a Lamborghini, take package holidays to the Med or splash out on exotic breaks, or prefer bingo to a Beethoven concert.

The industry's claims have been verified by sociologist Professor Roger Burrows, who told the Festival of Science this week that these profiles are 'frighteningly accurate'.

He cross-checked the Experian computer profiles against the reality on the street in the small East Yorkshire town of Howden, together with a street in Hoxton, East London.

The professor found that the postcode profiles matched near-perfectly with the properties and lifestyles he observed.

'In Howden, all the houses were similar, but you could almost feel the crack in the street where the postcode started to change,' he said. 'Cars in the drive started to change, and the wooden windows changed to UPVC.'

By Sean Poulter, Consumer Affairs Editor

Companies can buy access to the MOSAIC database and similar systems, such as ACORN, to decide where to target the marketing of goods and services.

Supermarkets use the information to find the best location to site a new store, while insurance companies can use life expectancy details or claims information to decide how to price their policies. Political parties have bought access to the data in order to target mailshots to drum up support.

But Experian and its rivals deny there is anything sinister in this system of classifying the nation.

A spokesman said: 'People have got the wrong idea that this is all about helping companies decide whom they will send junk mail to. Nothing could be further from the truth. It is increasingly used as a tool by government and public bodies to target services to where they are needed.'

The technology allows the health service to plot which types, or tribe, of people are most likely to suffer from certain diseases, such as obesity-related diabetes.

In theory, it can then target resources and health information to the people who are most in need.

Similarly, the fire service has used the data to see what sort of people have made fire insurance claims in the past and so identify similar people who might do so in the future. It then targets fire prevention advice.

Cynics would point out that insurance companies will also use such information to push up premiums.

The profiles are said to be a factual assessment, but many are not complimentary and people will argue with the conclusions.

Whatever, they give a fascinating insight into how the postcode – originally designed to speed up postal deliveries – has become the new arbiter of social class.

⇨ This article first appeared in the *Daily Mail*, 13 September 2007.

© 2007 Associated Newspapers Ltd

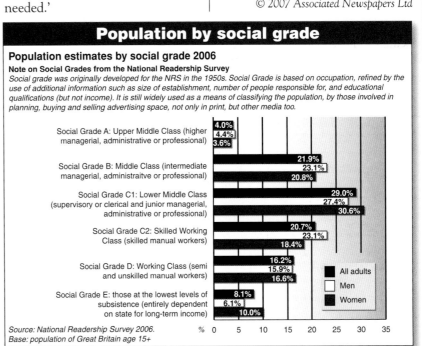

Population by social grade

Population estimates by social grade 2006

Note on Social Grades from the National Readership Survey
Social grade was originally developed for the NRS in the 1950s. Social Grade is based on occupation, refined by the use of additional information such as size of establishment, number of people responsible for, and educational qualifications (but not income). It is still widely used as a means of classifying the population, by those involved in planning, buying and selling advertising space, not only in print, but other media too.

Social Grade A: Upper Middle Class (higher managerial, administrative or professional) — 4.0% / 4.4% / 3.6%

Social Grade B: Middle Class (intermediate managerial, administraitve or professional) — 21.9% / 23.1% / 20.8%

Social Grade C1: Lower Middle Class (supervisory or clerical and junior managerial, administrative or professional) — 29.0% / 27.4% / 30.6%

Social Grade C2: Skilled Working Class (skilled manual workers) — 20.7% / 23.1% / 18.4%

Social Grade D: Working Class (semi and unskilled manual workers) — 16.2% / 15.9% / 16.6%

Social Grade E: those at the lowest levels of subsistence (entirely dependent on state for long-term income) — 8.1% / 6.1% / 10.0%

Legend: All adults / Men / Women

Source: National Readership Survey 2006.
Base: population of Great Britain age 15+

Social mobility in Britain

**Riven by class and no social mobility – Britain in 2007.
Information from the *Guardian***

⇨ *No change in 10 years of Labour rule.*
⇨ *89% say they are judged by class.*
⇨ *Poll shows deep North-South gap.*

Ten years of Labour rule have failed to create a classless society, according to a *Guardian*/ICM poll published today. It shows that Britain remains a nation dominated by class division, with a huge majority certain that their social standing determines the way they are judged.

Of those questioned, 89% said they think people are still judged by their class – with almost half saying that it still counts for 'a lot'. Only 8% think that class does not matter at all in shaping the way people are seen.

The poorest people in society are most aware of its impact, with 55% of them saying class, not ability, greatly affects the way they are seen.

Gordon Brown claimed at this year's Labour conference that 'a class-free society is not a slogan but in Britain can become a reality'. But even the supposedly meritocratic Thatcher generation of adults born in the 1980s appear to doubt that: 90% of 18- to 24-year-olds say people are judged by their class.

The poll also shows that after 10 years of Labour government, social change in Britain is almost static. Despite the collapse of industrial employment, the working class is an unchanging majority. In 1998, when ICM last asked, 55% of people considered themselves working class. Now the figure stands at 53%.

Of people born to working-class parents, 77% say they are working class too. Only one-fifth say they have become middle class.

Despite huge economic change and the government's efforts to build what it calls an opportunity society,

By Julian Glover

people who think of themselves as middle class are still in a minority. In 1998, 41% of people thought of themselves as middle class, exactly the same proportion as today. The upper class is almost extinct, with only 2% of those who answered claiming to be part of it.

> **Of those questioned, 89% said they think people are still judged by their class – with almost half saying that it still counts for 'a lot'**

The poll paints a picture of a nation divided by social attitudes and life-chances, with 47% of those living in south-east England considering themselves middle class, against 39% in the north and 35% in Wales and the west.

Northern England remains a working-class heartland, with 57% of people describing themselves as part of it.

Scots – 47% of whom think they are middle class – are just as class-bound as English citizens. Almost half of Scots say that class plays an important part in the way people are judged by others.

Social change is taking place slowly. The middle class has grown:

although 41% of people think they are part of it, only 32% say their parents were. In 1998, 69% of people thought their parents were working class. Now only 63% say so, and of those only 53% say they are working class themselves. That shift mirrors the attitude of the former deputy prime minister John Prescott, who admitted 'I'm pretty middle class' despite his working-class origins.

But many class attitudes have survived economic change. That suggests people are still judged by where they come from rather than how much they earn.

⇨ ICM Research interviewed a random sample of 1,011 on October 17-18. Interviews were conducted across the country and the results have been weighted to the profile of all adults. ICM is a member of the British Polling Council and abides by its rules.
20 October 2007
© *Guardian Newspapers
Limited 2007*

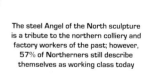

The steel Angel of the North sculpture is a tribute to the northern colliery and factory workers of the past; however, 57% of Northerners still describe themselves as working class today

Middle Britain

New *Middle Britain* report confirms rise of British middle class

⇨ *44% increase in number of middle class in last 40 years.*
⇨ *Over half of Britons still working class, but middle class to overtake by 2020.*
⇨ *£104,000 wealth gap between middle and working classes.*
⇨ *'Muddle class' Britain sees emergence of new class types.*
⇨ *Financial distinctions like savings, investments and property assets increase in importance as key class differentiators.*

The number of Britons who regard themselves as middle class has risen by nearly a half (44%) in the last 40 years, according to new research from Liverpool Victoria, the UK's largest friendly society.*

Although over half of the population say they are working class (53%), over four in ten Britons (43%) now see themselves as middle class

---

The new *Middle Britain* report shows that although over half of the population say they are working class (53%), over four in ten Britons (43%) now see themselves as middle class. This is a rise of 44% since 1966, when just 30% of the population regarded themselves as middle class. Moreover, the research predicts that by 2020 more UK adults will regard themselves as middle class than working class.

The report also reveals a huge wealth gap between the middle and working classes of over £104,000 in individual wealth, which means a massive wealth gap across the UK as a whole. This is despite the fact that working-class disposable incomes have risen considerably in the last 20 years, to the extent that even after discounting inflation they now exceed the level of middle-class incomes in the 1980s.

The new *Middle Britain* research report was conducted for Liverpool Victoria by independent think tank the Future Foundation, and comprises desk research from the British Household Panel Survey and the British Election Survey, plus new consumer omnibus research.

'Muddle class' Britain

The report also suggests that 'Muddle Class' (as opposed to middle class) Britain may be a more appropriate description of today's society, as some new class types are emerging that defy traditional class differentiators, namely:
⇨ ROBs (Rich Ordinary Britons) – the 2.67million people who regard themselves as working class even though their wealth ranks them in the top fifth of the population for asset wealth.

⇨ HEWs (High Earning Workers) – the half a million people in the UK (534,000) who earn over £100,000 per year in household income, yet still claim they are working class. The nation's HEWs are worth £53bn in total.
⇨ SALs (Suburban Asset Lightweights) – the 1.84 million people who call themselves middle class, yet are asset poor and in the bottom fifth of the population in terms of asset wealth.

The research also revealed a significant number of profession mismatches, such as the 36% of builders regarding themselves as middle class, and the three out of ten bank managers (29%) who see themselves as working class.

Traditional class differentiators changing

The report also shows that the traditional class markers such as family background, education and job, whilst still important, are being joined by savings, investments and property indicators. There are also some differences in perception between the middle and working classes as to what constitute the key class markers.

The working classes rate income as a more important factor than do the middle classes, whereas the latter regard education and housing as more significant than do their working class counterparts.

Finance and social class

How the assets add up

	Middle class	Working class	Difference
Income	£25,485	£20,553	£4,932
Investments	£7,672	£2,688	£4,984
Savings	£7,878	£4,081	£3,797
Property	£220,000	£129,000	£91,000
Debt	(£3,267)	(£2,770)	(£497)
Total	**£257,768**	**£153,552**	**£104,216**

Source: Middle Britain, Liverpool Victoria and the Future Foundation

Income and debt

According to the *Middle Britain* report, the average middle-class full-time worker earns a quarter more annually than their working-class counterpart, £25,485 compared with £20,553. However, age is important here, as up to age 24 the average working-class income is 16% higher. However, after age 45 the middle classes begin to cash in on their status, earning 54% more than their working-class equivalents at this age.

The higher middle-class earnings may be due in part to better education, as they are four times more likely to have a degree than the working classes.

The majority of chief income earners work in non-manual jobs, showing a shift away from the traditional association of the working class with manual jobs.

Interestingly, the report also shows that the working classes believe they work hardest for their money.

On debt, the *Middle Britain* report shows that the average amount of debt (excluding mortgage debt) owed by the middle classes is £3,267 and by the working classes is £2,770, although the overall debt burden for the latter is greater due to their lower income.

Savings and investments

The middle classes have twice as much as their working-class counterparts in savings and almost three times as much in investments (e.g. stocks and shares). Attitudes towards savings also differ markedly between the classes, with the working classes seeming to take a shorter-term approach.

Only one in five of the working class say they save for the long term, compared with three out of ten middle-class people. Also, whilst one in three of the middle classes are saving for their retirement, this falls to one in five for the working classes.

When it comes to spending, half of the working classes say they live for the moment (48%), compared with less than a third of the middle classes (29%).

Middle-class meanies

The middle classes are twice as mean with their money as the working classes. According to the Liverpool Victoria survey, 23% of middle-class respondents admitted to being mean with their money, compared with just 12% of working-class respondents saying the same.

A nation of homeowners

The *Middle Britain* report indicates a similar level of home ownership between the classes (84% among middle and 75% among working classes) but middle-class homes are worth some 70% more than working-class equivalents. In addition, four in ten of the middle classes own their home outright, with no mortgage, compared with less than three in ten for the working classes.

⇨ The average value of a middle-class home is £220,000, 70% higher than that of a working-class home (£129,000).

⇨ The percentage of middle-class homeowners (including mortgagors) is 84.4%, 12.5% higher than among the working classes (75%).

⇨ The middle classes are 77% more likely to own a home outright than the working classes (39.5% of middle classes own a home outright, compared with 28.8% of the working class).

How the assets add up

Nigel Snell, Liverpool Victoria's Head of Corporate Communications, said: 'Classical definitions of class are changing, with financial measures such as income, investments and property assets becoming as significant as where you live or your education.

'The wealth gap between the classes is significant and may be compounded by the shorter-term attitude to saving and slightly higher debt burden of the working classes. Saving regularly for the future is something that we should all be doing more of and we would encourage everyone to try to put something by, if only a little and often, to help build up a nest egg for the future.'
* *Association of Friendly Societies Year Book 2005/2006, total net assets.*
5 May 2006

⇨ The above information is reprinted with kind permission from Liverpool Victoria and the Future Foundation. Visit www.futurefoundation.net for more information.
© *Liverpool Victoria/Future Foundation 2006*

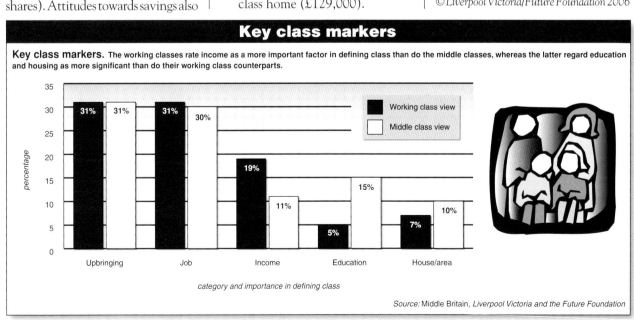

Key class markers

Key class markers. The working classes rate income as a more important factor in defining class than do the middle classes, whereas the latter regard education and housing as more significant than do their working class counterparts.

Legend: ■ Working class view □ Middle class view

category	Upbringing	Job	Income	Education	House/area
Working class view	31%	31%	19%	5%	7%
Middle class view	31%	30%	11%	15%	10%

category and importance in defining class

Source: Middle Britain, *Liverpool Victoria and the Future Foundation*

Social mobility

Information from the Economic and Social Research Council

Absolute and relative mobility

Social scientists refer to two varieties of social mobility.

Absolute mobility is the aggregate of individuals' movement through the socio-economic structure of a society over time. It is measured by comparing the social class origin of an individual (usually determined by their parents' social class) against their social class 'destination' as an adult. Absolute mobility can increase if there are changes to the occupational structure as a whole.

Relative mobility considers how the chance of being socially mobile varies according to starting position. In a meritocratic society it is expected that the chance of attaining a particular place in the occupational class structure will not be strongly determined by one's social class origin.

Social class overview

The chart over the page shows the distribution of occupations of the adult population in the UK according to the National Statistics Socio-economic classifications (NS-SEC).

There was significant structural change in occupational social class during the 20th century. Manual occupations shrank from nearly three-quarters of the workforce in 1911 to around 38 per cent in 1991. They were displaced by growth in managerial, professional and clerical jobs.

These changes are reflected in mobility rates. Of men born between 1950 and 1959, 42 per cent were upwardly mobile compared to their fathers, but only 13 per cent downwardly mobile. The equivalent figures for women were 36 per cent and 27 per cent respectively, although the latter figure may be an over-statement since it would be more accurate to compare women to their mothers than their fathers.

Sociologists have found that there has previously been little 'long-range' mobility in Britain with people born between 1900 and 1960. An Oxford University study reported that only around 10 per cent of boys from working-class backgrounds ended up in the 'service class', with a similar proportion of sons of service-class fathers ending up in the working class. The service class is a term used by some sociologists to describe the upper middle class of management and professional occupations.

These patterns of low social mobility are still common to most Western industrial societies. In their book *The Constant Flux*, Robert Erikson and John Goldthorpe show how, despite substantial changes in the class structure of major European nations, the USA, Australia and Japan, the relative chance of social mobility remains remarkably constant.

Women's mobility

Over the 20th century, women in the workforce grew substantially. Women have grown as a proportion of the workforce from 29 per cent in 1900 to 46 per cent in 2000. Whereas around five million women were working in 1900, in 2000 there were 13 million in employment. This is perhaps the most significant change in the occupational class structure since 1900 and presented women with opportunities for social mobility that had not previously been widely available. Women currently make up 46 per cent of the population.

Ethnic minorities are more likely to be socially mobile (in both directions) than the white population

Women are concentrated in particular occupations in the UK labour market. 79 per cent of administrative and secretarial workers are women, as are 83 per cent of personal service workers. However, only nine per cent of skilled trades employees are female. Women comprise 31 per cent of managers and senior officials.

There remains something of a 'glass ceiling' for women in access to the very top positions in British society, as shown in table 1 over page.

Ethnic minorities' social mobility

Immigrants to the UK have historically been downwardly mobile. Many first-generation Commonwealth migrants during the twentieth century were forced to take manual jobs in the UK having held white-collar positions in their country of birth.

Ethnic minorities are more likely to be socially mobile (in both directions) than the white population. Whereas 57 per cent of the white population were found not to be mobile in a longitudinal census study, this dropped to 42 per cent for those of Indian origin and 37 per cent for Pakistanis, both groups seeing broadly equal rates of upward and downward mobility.

The chart below shows the composition of class origins for different ethnic groups. Note that the social class definitions used are slightly different – here is the scheme used by CREST. There are many different schemes in existence.

Mobility and inequality

Since 1974 there has been a growth in household income inequalities. In 1974 the 10 per cent of households with the highest incomes had, on average, three times the income of the lowest 10 per cent, by 2001/2 the gap had increased so that the richest households had four times the income of the poorest. This was despite the poorest households seeing a 30 per cent increase in their income in real terms.

Inequalities in wealth remain fairly constant over time. The proportion of the UK's marketable wealth owned by the most wealthy 1 per cent is 21 per cent of all wealth. At the same time, the proportion of marketable wealth owned by the least wealthy 50 per cent is only 7 per cent of the total UK.

Chief executives of the FTSE 100 (top 100 listed companies) earn on average £730,796 per year, an increase of nearly three times their average earnings in 2000. The median UK annual salary is approximately £25,000. A full-time employee earning the minimum wage (£5.35 for over 22s) would have earned around £9,000 for the year.

Factors affecting social mobility

Education is the main determinant of whether or not one is upwardly mobile. British sociologists tend to agree that credentials have replaced social class origin per se as the best predictor of attaining a service-class position. However, there are unequal success rates between social classes at school and unequal entry and success rates in post-compulsory education.

Socio-economic class is shown to vary participation rates in post-compulsory education. 74 per cent of students whose parents were those from a higher professional social class background were studying for GCE A-levels or equivalent, compared with 31 per cent of those whose parents are from a routine occupation.

A study found that around 10 per cent of university graduates are in the same occupation as their father, with around 30 per cent in the same occupational group. Direct occupational inheritance is strongest in medicine and agriculture.

...and finally

Since its launch in 1994, the National Lottery has created over 1,900 new millionaires. Those most likely to experience this unusual form of social mobility include builders, machine operators and administrators/office workers.

Updated 6 December 2006

⇨ The above information is re-printed with kind permission from the Economic and Social Research Council. Visit www.esrcsocietytoday. ac.uk for more information or to view notes and references.

© ESRC

Social mobility – statistics

Figure 1: All in employment by socio-economic classification (NS-SEC), winter 2005/06

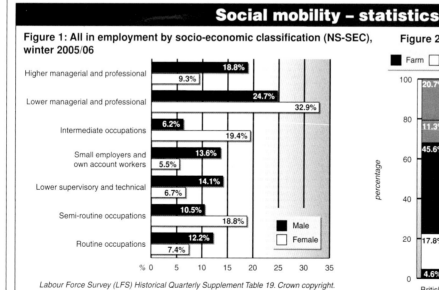

Labour Force Survey (LFS) Historical Quarterly Supplement Table 19. Crown copyright.

Figure 2: Class origins by ethnic group

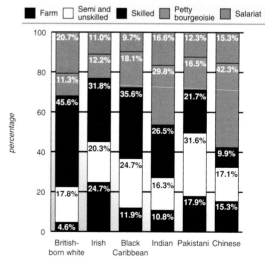

Source: Ethnic differences in the labour market (1999), CREST.

Table 1: Percentage of women in Britain's top jobs

Occupation/role	% female	Occupation/role	% female
MP (House of Commons)	20	High Court judge	7
MSP (Holyrood)	37	FTSE 100 company CEO	1
MEP (Strasbourg)	24	FTSE 100 company director	7
MWA (Cardiff)	50	University Professor	14
Local Authority councillor	30	Church of England bishop	0

Source: multiple sources. See ESRC factsheet 'Social Mobility', reference 9, for list (www.esrcsocietytoday.co.uk/ESRCInfoCentre/facts/index24.aspx?ComponentId=7095&SourcePageId=7074)

Statistics taken from the Economic and Social Research Council factsheet 'Social Mobility'

Social contrast

New atlas of identity in Britain reveals stark social contrasts

Researchers at the University of Sheffield have created an innovative atlas which provides clear proof that most of Britain is not the diverse country many believe it to be, showing a startling lack of social integration and social mobility.

Identity in Britain: A cradle-to-grave atlas, published by the Policy Press, is the first atlas to show how life in Britain varies over seven life stages and according to where we live. It compares over 1,000 neighbourhoods, in terms of people and identities rather than geography.

Dr Bethan Thomas, from the University's Department of Geography and co-author of the report, said: 'Our conclusion is that Britain is becoming increasingly segregated across all ages by class, education, occupation, home ownership, health status, disability and family type. There is much more to identity in Britain than identities of religion and ethnicity. Mapping at different ages shows ever more clearly that where you live can limit or assist your life chances from the cradle to the grave.'

The atlas shows that our definition of 'normal' varies depending on where we live and that many of us don't understand that other people's idea of what is normal may be different to ours. It examines what normal means in different neighbourhoods through the seven stages of life.

The key findings are:

⇨ In the first stage of life (under five) there are no large neighbourhoods where children in the highest social class mix with any other class of children other than the one just beneath them. Infants living in social housing are likely to find themselves in over-crowded homes whilst those whose parents are home owners are often growing up in small palaces with a surfeit of rooms.

⇨ In the second stage of life (5 to 15) the proportion of school-aged children living with a step-parent varies from less than one in twenty in towns and cities, to almost one in five in rural areas. The average child in the wealthiest 10% of neighbourhoods can expect to inherit at least 40 times the wealth of the average child in the poorest 10%.

⇨ Young adults in the third stage of life (16 to 24) in the poorest neighbourhood are nearly 20 times more likely not to be in education, employment, or training than those in the wealthiest neighbourhood. In contrast, 50 times more young people from some neighbourhoods enrol at an elite university than others. There are a few large neighbourhoods where not a single child goes to an elite university.

⇨ During the fourth stage of life (25 to 39), up to two-thirds of mid-lifers in some neighbourhoods have children, while in others, as few as one in seven do. Thus, whether it is normal to have children at these ages now depends on where you live. In every large neighbourhood in Britain, where the majority of mid-lifers are in professional occupations (AB), the next largest number is in social marketing group C1. Even at these ages, there is not a single large neighbourhood in Britain that could be described as mixed by social grade.

⇨ In the fifth stage of life (40 to 59) up to three times as many mature people are separated, divorced or remarried as in others and there is a clustering of this group towards the coasts. There almost half of people were once married. Although many people will have first taken out a 25-year mortgage in their 20s, in only half a per cent of all neighbourhoods do a majority actually own their property outright.

⇨ The sixth stage of life (60 to 74) most clearly illustrates the differences between living in poor and wealthy neighbourhoods. Far more men than women can drive. Many old men live in households with access to two or more cars, but far fewer old women do. In a third of neighbourhoods the health of most is only fair, and in a handful of neighbourhoods it is considered normal to be in poor health.

⇨ In the seventh and final stage of life (75 until death) there are more widows than widowers because men die earlier than women. 20%-44% of men and 45%-74% of women have been widowed and not remarried. In every neighbourhood in Britain over the last 24 years, at least one person has lived to be 100, but in some neighbourhoods very many more reach their centenary. All in all, the atlas provides a myriad of illuminating insights into the neighbourhood geographies of identity and the opportunities and disadvantages associated with living in particular places.

Professor Daniel Dorling, added: 'Most people think they are average when asked. In most things most are not. Most say they are normal, but our atlas shows that what is normal changes rapidly as you travel across the social topography of human identity in Britain, from the fertile crescent of advantage, where to succeed is to do nothing out of the ordinary, to the peaks of despair, where to just get by is extraordinary.'
10 September 2007

⇨ The above information is reprinted with kind permission from the Policy Press. Visit www.policypress.org.uk for more information.

© *Policy Press*

The class debate demands to be heard

'The reality is that class still has a strong bearing on people's sense of how they orientate themselves in society'

By Madeleine Bunting

One of the most pervasive myths about Britain in recent times has been that of the 'classless society'. A series of politicians have made great claims of a meritocratic culture, but the recent findings on social mobility dented the credibility of such ideas as it showed how social-economic status at birth was becoming a stronger indicator of your life course than ever.

Here comes another nail in the coffin of what we would like to believe about Britain. The latest edition of *British Social Attitudes*, published today, shows that the British are just as likely as ever to identify themselves as belonging to a class. In 1964, 47% of people ascribed themselves to a class unprompted, and in 2005 that figure was 45%. Another 47% and 49% respectively did likewise when prompted by the researcher. A minuscule 6% said they did not identify with any class. So class is just as meaningful a term as it ever was.

But while the incidence of class identity has barely budged, the proportions claiming to be middle class have significantly increased over the 40-year period – as one would expect, given the spread of higher education and growth in white-collar jobs. In fact, according to those latter measures, more should be claiming middle-class status than do. Qualitative research showed up how people continue to use a class identity of upbringing, long after they have achieved a different social-economic status.

What the research challenged was the influential thesis of sociologist Ulrich Beck that traditional collective identities have been 'dissolved in the acid bath of competition' and that, in their place, people have had to create their own 'life-worlds: without communal reference points'.

This was the brave new world of individualisation. But the research does not support the thesis.

One of the most pervasive myths about Britain in recent times has been that of the 'classless society'

The reality is that class still has a strong bearing on people's sense of how they orientate themselves in society; it helps them answer questions such as 'Who is like me?' and 'Who do I feel comfortable with?' Class still operates just as powerfully in people's subjective perception of their circumstances. What has changed is whether this sense of emotional identification translates into agreed mutual interests – a political as well as emotional solidarity. This is where the change is pronounced: the link between class and politics has almost completely broken down.

It is striking that a concept as prevalent as class is so rarely discussed. It has become the last taboo. We have become used to discussing status but the ways in which class awards those key characteristics for social mobility of cultural advantage and a sense of entitlement have been neglected. Without an understanding of how class reproduces itself generation after generation, our grasp of why working-class children fail to match the educational achievements of their middle-class counterparts remains inadequate.

In the past year, a group of new writers has been striding into the territory, trying to find a way to describe this subjective, personal experience of class and how it shapes a sense of self. Lynsey Hanley writes about the experience of growing up on a Birmingham council estate in her recent book, *Estates*; Libby Brooks, in *The Story of Childhood: Growing Up in Modern Britain*, analyses modern childhood; and philosopher Julian Baggini, in his new book, *Welcome to Everytown*, examines life in Rotherham beyond the comfortable self-assurance of metropolitan middle England.

It is no easy task. As one of these writers, Gillian Evans, wrote in *Society* last autumn, 'the relationship between social classes in England hinges on a segregation that is emotionally structured through mutual disdain'.

⇨ Madeleine Bunting is a *Guardian* columnist. She chaired a *Guardian* Newsroom event, The Last Taboo: Class in Britain, with Lynsey Hanley, Libby Brooks and Alexander Masters, on 1 February 2007.

24 January 2007

Social mobility in advanced countries

Disturbing finding from LSE study – social mobility in Britain lower than other advanced countries and has declined

⇨ *In a comparison of eight European and North American countries, Britain and the United States have the lowest social mobility.*

⇨ *Social mobility in Britain has declined.*

⇨ *Part of the reason for Britain's decline has been that the better off have benefited disproportionately from increased educational opportunity.*

Researchers from the Centre for Economic Performance at the London School of Economics and Political Science (LSE) have compared the life chances of British children with those in other advanced countries for a study sponsored by the Sutton Trust, and the results are disturbing.

Jo Blanden, Paul Gregg and Stephen Machin found that social mobility in Britain – the way in which someone's adult outcomes are related to their circumstances as a child – is lower than in Canada, Germany, Sweden, Norway, Denmark and Finland. Of the countries considered, the US and UK were at the bottom of the mobility league, this general pattern is confirmed by results from a number of other studies.

Social mobility in Britain is lower than in Canada, Germany, Sweden, Norway, Denmark and Finland

Comparing surveys of children born in 1958 and 1970, the researchers were able to compare changes in mobility over time in the UK and found that the earnings of those born in 1970 were more closely related to their parental income than those born in 1958. Britain's falling mobility was found to be explained, in part, by the strong and increasing relationship between family income and educational attainment.

Britain's declining mobility is in part due to the strong and increasing relationship between family income and educational attainment

For these children, additional opportunities to stay in education at age 16 and age 18 disproportionately benefited those from better off backgrounds. For a more recent cohort born in the early 1980s the gaps in staying on rates at 16 by parental income narrowed, but inequality of access to higher education has widened further: while the proportion of people from the poorest fifth of families obtaining a degree has increased from 6 per cent to 9 per cent between the early 1980s and late 1990s the graduation rates for the richest fifth have risen from 20 per cent to 47 per cent over the same period.

Sir Peter Lampl, chairman of the Sutton Trust, said: 'These findings are truly shocking. The results show that social mobility in Britain is much lower than in other advanced countries and is declining – those from less privileged backgrounds are more likely to continue facing disadvantage into adulthood, and the affluent continue to benefit disproportionately from educational opportunities. I established the Sutton Trust to help address the issue, and to ensure that all young people, regardless of their background, have access to the most appropriate educational opportunities, right from early years care through to university. *Adapted from a news release issued on 25 April 2005; updated 10 January 2008*

⇨ The Centre for Economic Performance is a research centre within the London School of Economics The above information is reprinted with kind permission from the LSE and has been adapted from an LSE news release. Visit www.lse.ac.uk for more information.

© London School of Economics

The tyranny of suburbia

How changing places is still a very middle-class thing

The class system is alive and well when it comes to people moving up the housing chain, according to a study funded by the Economic and Social Research Council (ESRC), which talks of 'the tyranny of suburbia'.

And while 'residential mobility' has increased dramatically since the mid-1970s, middle-class suburbanites have successfully imposed their 'tastes' onto the housing field, says research from Sheffield Hallam University, led by Professor Chris Allen.

Social scientists have argued that uprooting to live in a different area is caused by 'triggers' such as the decline of a neighbourhood. Conversely, immobility is said to be due to an absence of these triggers, or to constraints such as lack of money.

However, the new study, centred on a regeneration neighbourhood of Liverpool, found that attitudes to moving home were much more influenced by social class background.

In interviews with residents, directors of regeneration companies, local officials, community workers, estate agents and others involved, researchers identified two groups of household types. They dubbed these 'located' and 'cosmopolitan'.

Located residents were working class, and their main consideration was to get from 'day to day'. They judged their housing and neighbourhood on that basis, and did not even see themselves as being on a property ladder. Cosmopolitans were middle class and paid enough to be able to see beyond the need to survive from day to day.

Professor Allen, now based at Manchester Metropolitan University, said: 'Although "happy with their lot", located, or working-class residents saw the choice of where to live as only between the suburban ideal, which they could not have, and "everything else". They did not consider a strategic move to climb the housing ladder and reach suburbia eventually.

'This shows just how successful middle-class residents have been at imposing their tastes when it comes to the places we live in.' Professor Allen continued: 'In other words, located residents only desired what was for "other people" rather than "the likes of them", so they only valued what they could not have, and this worsened their chances of moving up.'

The class system is alive and well when it comes to people moving up the housing chain

---

Turning to the middle-class residents, or cosmopolitans, the study says that although less obsessed with the suburban ideal, some did aspire to suburbia, and saw living in the redevelopment area as a step towards it.

Professor Allen said: 'Freedom from the necessities of day-to-day survival enabled them to view the housing market as a landscape of social, economic and cultural "signals" that they interpreted and responded to with mobility.

'They liked the area, but were only "here for now". They were able to step back a bit and judge the place from a distance. And they valued it because of its location in terms of the city centre, and closeness to such places as restaurants and entertainment venues, even if parts of it were "scruffy".'

Working-class residents saw regeneration plans for the area for what was produced 'here and now', and they lamented the agencies involved for 'doing nothing'. Cosmopolitans, meanwhile, saw regeneration as adding to future potential, even if progress was slow.

However, Professor Allen points out: 'The tendency for middle-class households to add value to places on their way up the housing ladder actually destabilises their suburban ideal, and therefore the principles that govern the housing field. This raises questions about the unfolding nature of divisions among the middle classes.'
25 October 2006

⇨ The above information is re-printed with kind permission from the Economic and Social Research Council. Visit www.esrc.ac.uk for more information.
© ESRC

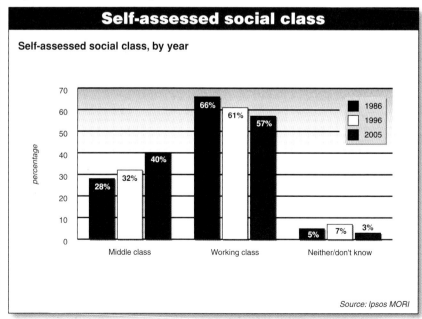

Self-assessed social class

Self-assessed social class, by year

Legend: 1986, 1996, 2005

Middle class: 28%, 32%, 40%
Working class: 66%, 61%, 57%
Neither/don't know: 5%, 7%, 3%

Source: Ipsos MORI

Inequality in Britain

New poverty and wealth maps of Britain reveal inequality to be at 40-year high

A new way of comparing poverty and wealth trends across Britain shows inequality has reached levels not seen for over 40 years. This is according to research released today (17 July) by the Joseph Rowntree Foundation. A second report, published simultaneously, has found that the public believes the gap between rich and poor people is too large.

Researchers working on the first report found that households in already-wealthy areas have tended to become disproportionately wealthier and that many rich people live in areas segregated from the rest of society. At the same time, more households have become poor over the last 15 years, but fewer are very poor.

Allowing more detailed comparisons than previously possible, the report contains comprehensive maps which are based on census and survey data illustrating the changes in poverty and wealth across Britain from 1968 to 2005.

The widening gap between rich and poor has meant that 'average' households (neither poor nor wealthy) have been decreasing in number. The report raises questions about what Britain will look like in ten years' time if trends continue as they have.

Danny Dorling, who led the research, said: 'Most interesting and certainly unexpected when this work began is the geography of those households who are neither rich nor poor. Over time it has become clear that there is less and less room in the south for them; they have either moved elsewhere, or become poor.'

The public believes the gap between rich and poor people is too large

The second report, from Michael Orton and Karen Rowlingson, studies people's attitudes to inequality. It found that over the last 20 years, a large and enduring majority of people have considered the gap between high and low incomes too large. However, people are more likely to think that those on higher incomes are overpaid, than to believe that those on low incomes are underpaid.

This report also found that despite most people considering the gap between rich and poor people to be too large, attitudes to wealth redistribution are complex. The authors conclude that while the public believe economic inequality is a problem, there is no clear public consensus about how this problem should be tackled.

Michael Orton said: 'There is evidence that a high level of inequality may cause real socio-economic problems. There is widespread acceptance that some occupations should be paid more than others: but the gap between high and low paid occupations is far greater than people think it should be.'

Notes

1. *Poverty, wealth and place in Britain 1968 to 2005* by Daniel Dorling, Jan Rigby, Ben Wheeler, Dimitris Ballas and Bethan Thomas from the University of Sheffield, Eldin Fahmy and David Gordon from the University of Bristol and Ruth Lupton from the University of London is published by the Policy Press. *Public attitudes to economic inequality* by Michael Orton from the University of Warwick and Karen Rowlingson from the University of Birmingham is published by the Joseph Rowntree Foundation.

2. The data on each area of the country and definitions of how the *Poverty, wealth and place in Britain* report defines poverty and wealth are available on http://www.sasi.group.shef.ac.uk/research/transformation/

17 July 2007

⇨ The above information is reprinted with kind permission from the Joseph Rowntree Foundation. Visit www.jrf.org.uk for more information.

© Joseph Rowntree Foundation

The work-rich/ work-poor society

Britain's growing polarisation between two-earner families and no-earner families

New research from the Institute for Social and Economic Research (ISER) highlights Britain's widening gap between 'work-rich' (two-earner) families and 'work-poor' (no-earner) families. While well-qualified couples in good health are increasingly likely to bring home two pay packets, disadvantaged couples are increasingly likely to have no job between them. And more single people are out of work.

Over the past 30 years, the proportion of adults with no direct or indirect access to an earned income has doubled from 7% to 14%. These no-earner families often depend on benefits, and have a high risk of income poverty – especially if they have children.

These findings confirm the government's emphasis on work as the most important route out of poverty – but they also show that the long-term trend has been in the wrong direction, even when the economy has been booming.

The study by ISER's Richard Berthoud was supported by the Joseph Rowntree Foundation. It provides a detailed analysis of the trends over the past 30 years.

The research finds that the number of people in employment is higher now than in the mid-1970s. But there have been substantial changes in the distribution of jobs between social groups:

⇨ Around two million adults (aged 20-59) who are in work today would probably not have had a job in the mid-1970s.

⇨ Those whose job prospects have improved most are mothers, especially those with adequate qualifications, good health and a working partner. (Mothers are still disadvantaged, but much less so than they were thirty years ago.)

⇨ This means that the number of couples who both have a job has increased. They are 'work-rich'.

⇨ On the other hand, there are another two million adults who probably would have had a job 30 years ago, but are now out of work.

⇨ Those whose chances have deteriorated most are disabled men with poor educational qualifications and no working partner.

While well-qualified couples in good health are increasingly likely to bring home two pay packets, disadvantaged couples are increasingly likely to have no job between them

---

⇨ There has been a steep increase, too, in the number of non-working adults without a partner or whose partner does not have a job. Most of these 'work-poor' families live on social security benefits, and have very low incomes.

⇨ These trends have not mainly been associated with changes in the demand for labour in the economy as a whole. But there are some signs that the underlying growth in the number of non-working families may have levelled off over the past few years.

These trends have had important consequences for equality and inequality. The report's author, Professor

Richard Berthoud, comments:

'Inequality (between men and women) within couple families has undoubtedly been reduced. Yet inequality between couple families has been increased by the two-earner/ no-earner polarisation.

'If part of the greater equality between husbands and wives consists of both of them having a job, another part consists of neither of them having a job. So inequality among women, and among men, may have increased.'

Notes

⇨ *Work-rich and Work-poor: Three decades of change* by Richard Berthoud is published for the Joseph Rowntree Foundation by the Policy Press (ISBN 978 1 86134 954 5, price £12.95). You can also download the Report, and a summary of the Findings, free from:
(Report) http://www.jrf.org.uk/ bookshop/details.asp?pubid=870
(Findings) http://www.jrf. org.uk/knowledge/findings/ socialpolicy/1996.asp

⇨ Richard Berthoud is research professor at the Institute for Social and Economic Research (ISER).

⇨ The research is based on new analysis of the General Household Survey conducted almost every year between 1974 and 2003.
28 March 2007

⇨ The above information is reprinted with kind permission from the Institute for Social and Economic Research. Visit www. iser.essex.ac.uk for more information.
© *ISER*

Gap between rich and poor narrows

Observations on equality

It looks as though, after drifting the wrong way for some years, Britain is gradually becoming a more equal society.

It looks as though, after drifting the wrong way for some years, Britain is gradually becoming a more equal society

New figures from the Office for National Statistics show that household income inequality fell in 2004/5 for the third year running, and post-tax inequality is now back at a level last seen in 1987. Even wealth inequality, which grew substantially over the past decade on the back of house-price increases, has pegged back.

But if the gap between rich and poor is generally narrowing, there are still plenty of people feeling little benefit. Hilary Armstrong, the new cabinet minister for social exclusion, says that at least a million people are firmly excluded from the mainstream. On a long list of

By Nick Pearce

indicators – the education of children in care, teenage pregnancy rates, mental health problems and weak basic skills in adults – the casualties keep coming.

Greater equality is not in itself a government objective. During the 2001 election campaign Tony Blair famously declared himself indifferent to David Beckham's earnings and said that tackling poverty, not reducing inequality, was his goal. In fact, he did both.

Old-fashioned tax and spend achieved a lot. Before tax and benefits do their redistributive work, the income of the top fifth of households is 16 times greater than that of the bottom fifth. After income transfers, the ratio is four to one. Progressive changes, such as generous tax credits and the rise in National Insurance to pay for the NHS, played an important part in reducing inequality. The minimum wage has also helped those at the bottom.

Child and pensioner poverty fell significantly, if not by as much as the government had planned. But a great deal of this success was with low-hanging fruit – families just below the poverty line. Entrenched exclusion is proving a harder nut to crack.

And despite the progress, the gap between rich and poor is still a lot wider than it was before Margaret Thatcher came to power, and wider than in most of Europe. In fact, a lot of the recent reduction simply made up for lost time in Labour's first term, when inequality worsened.

More worryingly, things are about to get harder. Spending growth will soon slow, the political space for tax or National Insurance increases has shrunk and the jobless count is going up. To reduce poverty and inequality will require some tough choices about spending priorities.

⇨ Nick Pearce is director of the Institute for Public Policy Research, which will publish a 'state of the nation' assessment of Labour's record in December.
29 May 2006

⇨ The above information is re-printed with kind permission from the *New Statesman*. Visit www.newstatesman.com for more information.

Education key to promoting social mobility

Information from the Department for Children, Schools and Families

Helping every child reach their full potential and closing the attainment gap between disadvantaged young people and their peers will be the top priority behind education policy, Alan Johnson, Secretary of State for Education and Skills, announced today.

In a wide-ranging speech he outlined plans to ensure every child – whatever their background – has the opportunity to fulfil their potential.

By 2010-11, the last year of the Spending Review period, the Department for Education and Skills will be investing over £1 billion more than today in closing the attainment gap and for the first time ever the Government plans to measure itself on how well it succeeds in its ambitions with a new public service agreement.

Research shows that a child from a disadvantaged background will have heard just 13 million words by the age of five compared to a child from a more affluent home who will have heard 45 million by the same age.

Children who are not in receipt of free school meals are twice as likely to get five good GCSEs than those who are and those from poorer backgrounds are also three times less likely to overcome a dip in their results.

As part of a package of measures being announced today to narrow the social class attainment gap, £217 million will be invested in 2010-11 so that disadvantaged young people will be able to access two hours a week of free after-school activities such as music, sport and drama as part of the extended schools programme. This will also fund some activities during the school holidays.

By 2010 all schools will be extended schools, offering activities from 8am to 6pm, five days a week, 48 weeks a year in response to demand. These will include homework clubs and study support and sport and music tuition.

Evidence shows extended schools bring benefits to vulnerable children and their families and offer the potential to intervene positively in the cycle of disadvantage. There is considerable evidence that extended provision can bring benefits to children's engagement in learning and self-esteem and early studies show relative improvements in attainment for this group.

Children who are not in receipt of free school meals are twice as likely to get five good GCSEs than those who are

---

Speaking at the ippr, Alan Johnson said:

'A number of complex factors determine a person's success in life. We must work on all of the different elements. But nothing plays a greater role in determining a child's future than their education.

'Historically, a high quality education only came with wealth; whilst social confidence came from social class. We've been determined that everyone should have the same opportunities as the affluent and this has meant elevating education right to the top of the political agenda.

'The progress we have made in education since 1997 – and particularly in schools in deprived areas – means that there is every reason to expect that today's generation of poor children will have much better chances to escape the limitations of their background.'

He added:

'Our challenge must be to continue to raise standards for all whilst closing the gap in attainment between those from deprived backgrounds and those from more affluent homes.

'A year ago, in my first major speech as Education Secretary, delivered to the Fabian Society, I announced that I would be looking closely at how we reduce the educational attainment gap.

'After a year's careful analysis, and with the CSR behind us, I'm delighted to announce a hefty package of measures, rising to more than a billion pounds a year by the end of this spending round, to address what Bevin called the poverty of aspiration. This new drive should be underscored and assessed with a new public service agreement goal to close the attainment gap.'

Alan Johnson also announced that by 2010-2011 the Government will spend over £1billion more on narrowing the attainment gap including:

⇨ ensuring the continued roll-out of Sure Start Children's Centres and providing special outreach workers in Sure Start Children's Centres in the most deprived regions;

⇨ emulating the successful London Challenge programme in two other cities;

⇨ paying for ten extra hours of tuition in English and Maths for the bottom 5 per cent of pupils to help 600,000 pupils when they fall behind;

⇨ expanding school-based mental health support; and

⇨ rolling out the Social and Emotional Aspects of Learning programme across all schools.

17 May 2007

⇨ The above information is reprinted with kind permission from the Department for Children, Schools and Families. Visit www.dcsf.gov.uk for more information.

Social mobility not improving

Low social mobility in the UK has not improved in 30 years

Social mobility in the UK remains at the low level it was for those born in 1970, with recent generations of children's educational outcomes still overwhelmingly tied to their parents' income, according to the latest Sutton Trust research released today.

The study, from the London School of Economics and the University of Surrey and funded by the Sutton Trust, reviews evidence related to children born between 1970 and the millennium, to determine whether the decline in social mobility between previous generations has continued.

The main findings of the work by Dr Jo Blanden and Professor Stephen Machin show that:

⇨ Intergenerational income mobility for children born in the period 1970 to 2000 has stabilised, following the sharp decline that occurred for children born in 1970 compared with those born in 1958.

⇨ However, the UK remains very low on the international rankings of social mobility when compared with other advanced nations.

⇨ Parental background continues to exert a very powerful influence on the academic progress of children.

⇨ Those from the poorest fifth of households but in the brightest group drop from the 88th per-centile on cognitive tests at age three to the 65th percentile at age five. Those from the richest households who are least able at age three move up from the 15th percentile to the 45th percentile by age five. If this trend were to continue, the children from affluent backgrounds would be likely to overtake the poorer children in test scores by age seven.

⇨ Inequalities in obtaining a degree persist across different income groups. While 44 per cent of young people from the richest 20 per cent of households acquired a degree in 2002, only 10 per cent from the poorest 20 per cent of households did so.

Sir Peter Lampl, Chairman of the Sutton Trust, commented:

'Shamefully, Britain remains stuck at the bottom of the international league tables when it comes to social mobility. It is appalling that young people's life chances are still so tied to the fortunes of their parents, and that this situation has not improved over the last three decades.

'We need a radical review of our approach to improving social mobility, starting with an independent commission to review the underlying causes for our low level of mobility and what can be done to address it.

This is an issue which requires action on a broad front over a long period – it is too important to be used as a political football.'

For its part, the Sutton Trust has been funding since 1997 a wide range of education access initiatives from the early years, through primary and secondary schools, to university and beyond. In partnership with the Carnegie Corporation of New York, the Trust is also hosting a high-level international summit to identify the drivers of social mobility and consider where governments and others should be focusing their efforts.

Dr Jo Blanden commented:

'By looking at the relationship between children's educational outcomes at different ages and parental income we can predict likely patterns of mobility for cohorts who have not yet reached adulthood. On this basis we cannot find any evidence that the sharp drop in mobility observed for children growing up in the 1970s and 1980s has continued. But nor can we find evidence that mobility has improved.'
13 December 2007

⇨ The above information is re-printed with kind permission from the Sutton Trust. Visit www.suttontrust.com for more information.
© *Sutton Trust*

It's official: class matters

A major new study shows that social background determines pupils' success. Does it mean that the government is heading in the wrong direction? Matthew Taylor reports

It is a familiar scene: mum and dad hunched at the kitchen table, poring over Ofsted reports and brochures, trying to fathom which is the best school for their child. But a new report, obtained by *Education Guardian*, suggests that these well-meaning parents, and thousands like them, are looking in the wrong place.

Instead of trying to decode inspectors' reports or work out whether academies are better than voluntary-aided schools or trusts superior to community comprehensives, they need look no further than the average earnings among parents.

A study by academics at University College London (UCL) and King's College London has given statistical backbone to the view that the overwhelming factor in how well children do is not what type of school they attend – but social class. It appears to show what has often been said but never proved: that the current league tables measure not the best, but the most middle-class schools; and that even the government's 'value-added' tables fail to take account of the most crucial factor in educational outcomes – a pupil's address.

The report, which uses previously unreleased information from the Department for Education and Skills, matches almost 1 million pupils with their individual postcode and exam scores at 11 and 15.

This unprecedented project has revealed that a child's social background is the crucial factor in academic performance, and that a school's success is based not on its teachers, the way it is run, or what type of school it is, but, overwhelmingly, on the class background of its pupils.

A study by academics has given statistical backbone to the view that the overwhelming factor in how well children do is not what type of school they attend – but social class

---

'These are very important findings, which should change the way parents, pupils and politicians think about schools,' says Richard Webber, professor at UCL. 'This is the first time we have been able to measure the precise impact of a child's social background on their educational performance, as well as the importance of a school's intake on its standing in the league tables.'

The findings come at a pivotal time in education with the government determined to push through its education reforms in a new schools bill, expected to be published today. If it is successful, all primary and secondary schools will be encouraged to become independent trusts with control over their own admissions. But many critics have argued that the government should be introducing more rigorous controls over admissions – to ensure as many

schools as possible have a balanced intake of middle- and working-class children.

The study found that, whatever their background, children do better the more 'middle-class' the school they attend, and also that more than 50% of a school's performance is accounted for by the social make-up of its pupils.

In affluent areas, such as Dukes Avenue, Muswell Hill, in north London, and Lammas Park Road, Ealing, west London, the study would expect 67% of 11-year-olds to achieve level 5 in the national English tests and 94% of 15-year-olds to get five or more passes at GCSE at grade C and above.

Meanwhile, of the children growing up in more deprived areas, such as Hillside Road, Dudley, or Laurel Road, Tipton (both in the West Midlands), just 13% are likely to get the top level 5 in the national English tests for 11-year-olds, while only 24% of 15-year-olds will be reckoned to achieve the benchmark five-plus GCSEs at grade C and above.

Put simply, the more middle-class the pupils, the better they do. The more middle-class children there are at the school, the better it does. It is proof that class still rules the classroom.

'The results show that the position of a school in published league tables, the criterion typically used by parents to select successful schools, depends more on the social profile of its pupils than the quality of the teachers,' says Webber, who, along with Professor Tim Butler from King's, has devised new school league tables from the data that take the social background of each pupil into account.

As it stands, parents who want to do the best for their children should choose a school according to how middle-class its intake is, rather than on the type of school or the quality of the teaching.

'For schools the message is clear. Selecting children whose homes are in high-status neighbourhoods is one of the most effective ways of retaining a high position in the league table. For statisticians, meanwhile, it proves that the existing tables, which ignore the types of home from which a school draws its pupils, are necessarily

an unfair and imprecise means of judging a school's achievements.'

The study looked at 476,000 11-year-olds and 482,000 15-year-olds. The data were analysed through Mosaic, a programme devised by the information company Experian, which divides the UK population by postcode into 11 main groups and 61 types, providing detailed insight into the socio-demographics, lifestyles, culture and behaviour of UK citizens. It is being used in key policy areas, such as health and crime, but this is the first time it has been used to assess the link between education performance and social class.

The study revealed how pupils from each of the 61 socio-economic groups performed given their background, allowing statisticians to set a benchmark score and measure each school's performance against that, in light of its intake. For this research Mosaic was linked to the Pupil Level Annual Statistics Data (National Pupil Database), provided by the DfES, to enable more accurate and context-based benchmarking of educational attainment.

The full report, which has yet to be given a title, will be published later this year and will be available from UCL.

Moving to a segregated system

Webber and Butler warn that introducing further freedoms for schools, as the government is, may allow middle-class parents and schools to choose each other, leaving those from poorer backgrounds stranded in an increasingly segregated system.

'Given the chance, a school will do as well as it can, and, as this research shows, that means attracting as many middle-class pupils as possible. Parents can see that their children will do better in the most middle-class schools, so they will strive to work the system to get in. So, by giving schools more independence and creating a market in education, you run the serious risk of polarising pupils along class lines,' says Webber.

He insists the government's attempts to introduce a market in education are also economically flawed: 'The beneficial peer group effects caused by the children of highly educated parents mean a market will not operate in the usual way. The best educational achievement for the largest number of pupils will be achieved by having a broad social mix of pupils in as many schools as possible. Some schools that currently draw their pupils from privileged social strata would lose out, but education standards would increase overall.'

Ministers who have gone cold on the idea of banding school admissions by ability in last year's white paper are unlikely to take much heed of the authors' concerns, but the new school league tables created by Webber and Butler are likely to raise further questions about the validity of the existing criteria for measuring success.

The tables, which work out how well schools should do in light of the social background of their intake, throw up differences with the scores produced by the DfES. In the primary school table, many previously middling schools come near the top of the pile. For secondary schools, the differences between the DfES's value-added figures and the alternative table are less pronounced. 'For the first time, we can see exactly how well schools are doing, taking into account the really crucial factor – the social background of their pupils,' said Webber. 'Previously even the value-added tables have failed to recognise the success of schools that serve very deprived communities. Conversely, some of the schools that are usually near the top in traditional tables are shown to be not quite as successful when you realise just how privileged their intake is.'

This is a view echoed – unsurprisingly – by Christine Haddock, headteacher at Larkspur community school in Gateshead – the most successful primary in the country according to the new league table.

'This is fantastic news,' Haddock told *Education Guardian*. 'We have always known that we are doing a good job for the children here, but the usual league tables rarely reflect that feeling.

'We serve a deprived area. In the last three years 46%-59% of our children have been eligible for free school meals [the standard indicator of deprivation]. But these findings reflect what we have always known: that this is a good school that looks after its pupils as well as it possibly can. Many of them are at quite a low level when they arrive, but they make massive strides before they leave.

'In the end, it's not about where you come in tables, it's about the difference that we can make to children's lives round here, but this will be a real boost to all the people who work so hard at the school.'

Another primary headteacher who welcomed the new league tables was Simon O'Keefe, headteacher of The Powell School in Dover, Kent, which came second in the country after not making the top 250 schools in the value-added rankings produced by the *Guardian* from the DfES performance tables.

'It is only in recent years that we are starting to feel we are getting recognition, but nothing like this,' says O'Keefe. 'It is obviously nice to feel we are successful in what we are trying to do here, but there is always room for improvement and, in the end, league tables are nice, but it is about teaching children to the best of our abilities so that they can reach their potential.'

The school has around 33% of pupils eligible for free school meals and a similar proportion with special educational needs. 'All our children, with perhaps one or two exceptions, come from the local council estate and from a fairly deprived background, but we have high expectations for them. We have high expectations of what they can achieve and of their behaviour. That, along with excellent teaching, is our fairly obvious secret.'

Questions for parents and schools

Among secondary schools, although many community schools with more socially deprived intakes make it into the top 200, some of the more traditional table-toppers still do well, particularly those from the grammar school sector.

Webber says this is because there is more selection at secondary schools, so they often cream off the more able pupils from disadvantaged areas while maintaining high results.

He adds that the research, including the new league tables, should be seen as the start rather than the end of an ongoing discussion.

'There are endless questions that this research throws up for parents and schools and, perhaps most crucially of all, for those making the decisions on where we go from here. Hopefully, this will begin a debate that will lead to a greater understanding of what is actually working in our schools and how best we can help children from all backgrounds achieve their potential.'

28 February 2006
© *Guardian Newspapers Limited 2006*

Keeping class out of the classroom

Information from *Education Today*

The Sutton Trust report was published last month and found that four-fifths of the private sector account for nearly one-third of all Oxbridge undergraduates each year.

One in six candidates starting at the UK's top two universities come from just 30 schools – of which just two are state grammars and one is a comprehensive. And the problem does not stop with Oxbridge. The report identified that a similar pattern could be found in admissions to other top UK universities, including Birmingham, Bristol, Durham, Edinburgh, Imperial and University Colleges, London, the London School of Economics, Nottingham, St Andrews, Warwick and York.

Sir Peter Lampl, Chairman of the Sutton Trust, whose aim is to provide educational opportunities for students from non-privileged backgrounds, said of the findings, 'It is deeply worrying – not to mention a sad waste of talent – that the chances of reaching one of these highly selective universities are much greater for those who attend a small number of the country's elite schools, mainly fee-paying.'

And on the surface these figures can be interpreted as an indictment against a class-ridden university application system, which favours middle-class students over those from poorer backgrounds. But a closer analysis of the situation reveals that numbers of applications to the top universities from state schools are falling. Could it be that the teaching profession is discouraging bright pupils from applying in the first place?

> **One in six candidates starting at the UK's top two universities come from just 30 schools – of which just two are state grammars and one is a comprehensive**

Oxbridge – the dreaming spires, punting and black-tie balls and bicycles piled high outside of lecture halls... The images are those of another era, of braying upper classes, wealth and privilege. Many students from state comprehensives would be forgiven for preferring the idea of some of the UK's other bastions of further education: such as Manchester, with its club culture, or Reading with its annual music festival. Without the support of their teachers to encourage them to aim for the top academic institutions, it is easy to see why applications are not forthcoming.

Then there is the applications procedure itself. While most universities will make a decision based on predicted grades at A Level alone when offering a place – Oxbridge demands a face-to-face interview. This is daunting enough for most candidates but less so for those who come from schools with a history of successfully submitting members of its student body. In these cases, a selection of students is routinely entered for Oxbridge every year and staff are familiar with the process.

So, are the top universities doing enough to break down these barriers that prevent state schools from entering their brightest students for consideration? An Oxford spokesman told the *Guardian* newspaper, 'Whilst a small number of schools do send a large number of pupils to apply to our university, the reverse is also true; a large number of schools send a small number of pupils. This shows that we are successfully reaching people in schools where the straight-A student is a minority.'

Cambridge, meanwhile, has 56 per cent of its student intake from state schools and spends £3m a year on initiatives to widen participation. 'Many of these... are yet to bear fruit. Others are aimed at raising aspirations generally and will not benefit Cambridge particularly,' the university claimed.

The Sutton Trust will spend £10m over the next five years to improve the aspirations of those applying

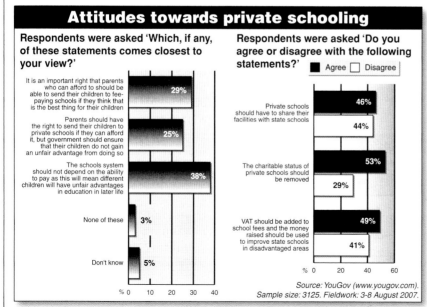

Attitudes towards private schooling

Respondents were asked 'Which, if any, of these statements comes closest to your view?'

- It is an important right that parents who can afford to should be able to send their children to fee-paying schools if they think that is the best thing for their children — 29%
- Parents should have the right to send their children to private schools if they can afford it, but government should ensure that their children do not gain an unfair advantage from doing so — 25%
- The schools system should not depend on the ability to pay as this will mean different children will have unfair advantages in education in later life — 38%
- None of these — 3%
- Don't know — 5%

% 0 10 20 30 40

Respondents were asked 'Do you agree or disagree with the following statements?' ■ Agree □ Disagree

- Private schools should have to share their facilities with state schools — Agree 46%, Disagree 44%
- The charitable status of private schools should be removed — Agree 53%, Disagree 29%
- VAT should be added to school fees and the money raised should be used to improve state schools in disadvantaged areas — Agree 49%, Disagree 41%

% 0 20 40 60

Source: YouGov (www.yougov.com). Sample size: 3125. Fieldwork: 3-8 August 2007.

for universities with ideas such as more summer schools for teenagers. Another idea mooted by the higher education minister Bill Rammell is a change to the current system of when students actually apply to university. At the moment this is done before the grades are known and decisions are made on predicted grades. It is plainly fairer for students to pitch their applications based on actual grades and allows the student greater confidence in aiming high in his or her choice of university.

Another slightly controversial proposal will come into effect from next year when students will be asked to indicate on their Ucas (university application form) whether their parents have a degree, with this information being passed on to admissions officers. Many are not sure about this initiative, which might be seen to favour those from backgrounds where there is no history of university attendance. A similar situation in the US designed to encourage greater numbers of ethnic minorities to pursue further education ended up being roundly criticised by both the middle classes who lost out on university places and those from ethnic minorities who resented the implication that they had not won their place on merit alone.

But there is also plenty that schools can do to ensure that their brightest pupils get a chance at the best universities. Clearly, it makes good business sense for private schools to boast to parents that they get a percentage of students into the top universities every year with several making it into Oxbridge. The pressure for state schools is often based on getting more students through exams with higher grades to ensure progress on the league tables. Therefore, a bright student might be encouraged to take those subjects most designed to offer a high return in terms of grade, for example media studies, than one that will be respected by one of the leading universities – such as history or a foreign language.

Bright students need to be identified when they are making their subject choices and encouraged to think that they can achieve their goals. But it appears that many teachers are concerned about raising expectations in students whose hopes may be dashed should they fail to win a place. A recent survey of teachers compiled by the National Foundation for Educational Research found that 80 per cent of teachers said, 'Able students from disadvantaged areas would find it difficult to cope socially (at Oxbridge).'

Equally worrying were the report's findings that teachers at state schools advising on university applications wrongly believed it cost more to attend Oxbridge and completely ignored information from these universities on bursaries.

On the surface these figures can be interpreted as an indictment against a class-ridden university application system

---

Could it be that there is inverted snobbery against these top educational institutions coming from some sectors of the state school system, which is also at the root of diminishing numbers of student applications? Certainly there appears to be a reluctance to pick out those brightest members of the classroom for anything that could be classed as special treatment.

Last year, the Government asked schools to identify those among the student body who would most benefit from higher education but 20 per cent failed to do so. A census of nearly 3,400 secondary schools in England by the Department for Education and Skills also carried out last year showed that a fifth believed they had no gifted pupils at all. A third of secondary schools had failed to register any pupils with the special academy that helps with specialist tuition, online educational packages, residential courses and summer schools on university campuses.

Could it all come down to cost? After all, the Government did introduce £3000 fees last year. But Mr Rammell claims that figures show this has not deterred students from poor backgrounds from applying to university per se.

Instead it appears to be a case of perception: with students from the state sector, their parents and teachers believing that the top universities are not suitable or attainable. While nobody is saying that Britain's many other universities do not provide a perfectly adequate form of higher education, it does seem a crying shame that some of the UK's students are being denied the opportunity to attend world-class institutions such as Oxford or Cambridge University because of lack of accurate information. Isn't it time to bury these outmoded class restrictions? They certainly have no place in the classroom.
November 2007

⇨ The above information is reprinted with kind permission from *Education Today*. Visit www.education-today. co.uk for more information.
© *Education Today*

Education is the only way to close class divide

By Janet Daley

So the England rugby fans apparently managed to find their way out of Paris without wrecking a single bar, overturning a single car or bottling a single South African supporter – let alone waging a pitched battle on the Champs-Elysées with a squad of armoured police.

Even those who arrived without tickets, drank with abandon and were reduced to sleeping rough in the streets – a sure-fire prescription for carnage if this had been a football World Cup – made no trouble for the authorities.

There are a few commentators who staunchly insist that this is not about class: that the difference between what Dave Tattoo and his mates would have done to Paris after losing a football World Cup final, and what the sad but non-violent rugby fans did, is nothing to do with the ugly social divide that still pervades Britain.

Well, delude yourself if you like – but this is about class. What confuses the issue now is that class is not all about money. Many thugs who travel abroad in fervent pursuit of the ultimate football fan's trophy – a charge of grievous bodily harm – are high earners, at least by the standards of their parents' generation. (After all, how else could they afford the trip?)

But what is so devastatingly depressing is that the class barrier in Britain is so immutable that even relative affluence cannot touch what lies at the heart of it. Since I arrived in this country, there has been a succession of optimistic prophecies about the end of the class system. When I got here in the 1960s you were in the midst of one: a great wave of creativity had arisen from the proletarian provinces – John Lennon and David Hockney, John Osborne and Kingsley Amis.

Surely this was the dawn of a new age of egalitarian meritocracy in which it was positively fashionable to have working-class roots? Look at the photographs of the England football team who won the World Cup in 1966. How respectable and middle class they appear – and how gentlemanly was their behaviour on the pitch by comparison to the rich sociopaths who now dominate the game.

Whatever happened to the decency and civility that was personified by Bobby Moore and the Charlton brothers? What happened to the desire of young working-class men to rise above the violence and borderline criminality that lay in wait for people of their backgrounds whose self-discipline was allowed to slip?

What confuses the issue now is that class is not all about money

It disappeared under a new wave of garbage culture and what seemed to me – a shocked outsider – like a positive conspiracy to maintain the separateness of working-class life, engineered jointly by sentimental media hokum and patronising middle-class guilt.

Whole genres of television programmes, whole tranches of truly appalling down-market magazines appeared on the scene, all apparently designed to celebrate the most degrading forms of working-class life. And as cynical and manipulative as these cold-blooded marketing exercises were, to criticise them was to invite charges of snobbery: as if no form of 'entertainment', however debased, should be regarded as too low to be an insult to this audience.

Schooling, which should have been the real answer to it all, was dominated by an educational establishment steeped in bourgeois guilt. I can remember having heated arguments with teachers and education officials who were adamant that children's ungrammatical regional dialects should not be corrected.

Do independent schools such as Eton and Harrow (pictured) emphasise the class divide?

'Correct' English, they insisted, was just a middle-class fetish which should not be imposed on children from 'other' backgrounds. So generations of working-class children had their feet set in social and cultural concrete by schools that refused to teach them how to speak and write their own language properly.

It happened again and again: in the 1980s there was another burst of meritocratic aspiration which saw a further wave of people break free from the limitations of their backgrounds – only to be ridiculed as 'Essex men' whose vulgar tastes and flashy wives still put them beyond the pale no matter how much they earned.

Now we have a new incarnation of the old division with 'chavs' and reborn Sloane Rangers. And a poll at the weekend states that 89 per cent of respondents believe that people in Britain are still judged by their class.

The Labour Government, convinced (rightly) that education is the answer to this, is trying to force universities to accept students whose schooling has been so inadequate that they cannot even achieve the low level of qualification needed to be admitted legitimately.

Social engineering is too subtle a term for this distortion of university entrance criteria: it is not so much a bending of the system as a bludgeoning that threatens to devalue what makes higher education so worthwhile. If education is the answer, then it must be allowed to do what only education can do: provide the rite of passage to an examined life.

That life requires an attitude which takes self-respect and the value of personal achievement for granted. Implant and nurture those things and the rest – aspiration, motivation and social mobility – will follow.

In Danny Danziger's book *Museum*, a collection of essays by people who work at New York's Metropolitan Museum of Art, there is a revelatory chapter by the head of security. The uniformed guards in the galleries at the Met are all graduates. This may be why they exercise far more discipline over the groups of schoolchildren than their British equivalents do: first, they feel more real commitment to the art, and second, they see no reason why everyone – from whatever background – should not be expected to behave in a museum.

Two of them became so involved with the objects they were guarding that they went back to university to get higher degrees and became museum curators. Ask yourself what the chances would be of that happening here, and even what response there would be to the suggestion that all museum guards should have higher education?

Forgive the homily, but it seems to be necessary to say this: self-respect comes to people from the expectations of others.

If you, as a society, do not expect correct speech, decent behaviour and a sense of responsibility from some of your fellow citizens – do not, in other words, demand from them what civilised life requires – then you deny them the chance to enter that life more effectively than if you had barred the gates to every centre of learning in the land.

22 October 2007
© *Telegraph Group Limited, London 2007*

Britain's teenagers' social skills gap widens

Information from the Institute for Public Policy Research

It is no longer enough for young people to rely on qualifications, according to new research from the Institute for Public Policy Research (ippr) published today (Mon). It shows that the shift to a service economy has made the acquisition of personal and social skills more important than ever before.

ippr's analysis of surveys with people born in 1958 and 1970 shows that personal and social skills – like communication, self-esteem, planning and self-control – became 33 times more important, between generations, in determining earnings later in life. Poor children who have high levels of application and concentration are 14 per cent more likely to be well-off by age 30, than the average poor child. The report shows social mobility has stalled. Twenty-two per cent of the decrease in social mobility was because working-class kids lacked personal and social skills.

But the report says qualifications still matter. GCSEs add around 10 per cent to wages compared to those with no qualifications, A-levels add a further 15 per cent for women and 20 per cent for men and a degree adds a further 25 per cent for women and 15 per cent for men.

The report says the best way for children to learn the skills that they need outside the family is through structured activities where they mix with children of other ages and backgrounds but are mentored by adult activity leaders and work towards specific goals. Examples include the Scouts, Cadets, martial arts, drama clubs and sporting teams.

Nick Pearce, ippr Director, said: 'There have always been class divides in education. But in the post-war period there were no social class gaps in how children were socialised into developing personal and social skills. Now there is a personal skills class divide and it is contributing in the decrease in social mobility.

'Adolescence is also being stretched at both ends, with children becoming "teenagers" earlier and

"adults" later. For too many young people this transition to adulthood is complex, messy and unsuccessful.'

The report concludes that learning 'soft skills' has become more important because of:

⇨ The structure of firms and the shift towards a service economy, which has led to an increase in both high skilled and low skilled 'technology-proof' jobs that cannot be outsourced.

⇨ Greater choice of different courses in further and higher education than ever before.

⇨ A shift in public policy, which has emphasised choice, voice, personalisation and individual customised public services.

⇨ Widening inequality in the 1980s and stalling social mobility, which have increased the gap between the best and worst-off.

ippr's report, *Freedom's Orphans: Raising Youth in a Changing World*, recommends:

⇨ Participation of every secondary school pupil (from 11 to 16 years old) in at least two hours a week of structured and purposeful extracurricular activities – such as martial arts, drama clubs, sports, cadets and Scouts. This would take place through extended school hours of between 8am and 6pm and would involve a legal extension of the school day. Parents who did not ensure their child attended two hours a week of activities might ultimately be fined, in the same way as parents are punished for their child's persistent truancy.

Twenty-two per cent of the decrease in social mobility was because working-class kids lacked personal and social skills

---

⇨ More school 'house systems' and more multi-age classes to strengthen children's self-esteem and help develop their social skills.

⇨ A ban on commercial television and print media advertising designed to capture the attention of children of primary school age. This will be a first step, while further consultation should be encouraged to determine the appropriate age limit.

⇨ A ban on commercial advertising through mobile phone and 3G platforms to handsets registered to children of primary school age. Parents should have the option of registering phone numbers with a dedicated body to ensure this happens.

⇨ Monitoring by Ofsted of commercial advertising in primary schools and other educational institutions for the primary age group must be carefully monitored.

⇨ Investment in a range of relationship support services for parents and couples, particularly lone parents. This needs to include new skills for professionals as part of workforce development in the NHS and social services, to enable them to identify and respond to relationship difficulties in couples.

⇨ Inclusion of couple relationship support training and training on working with men and fathers in social worker, health visitor and perinatal training and development, and a pilot scheme to test supportive interventions.

⇨ Development of information and support services for fathers at key transition points, notably in perinatal services and during separation.

⇨ Establishment of a UK cohort study to explore how relationships within families can best be supported by policy.

⇨ Roll-out of community-based perpetrator programmes for fathers with violent behaviour.

⇨ A role for the Child Support Agency in supporting families through divorce and separation. This should be modelled on the Australian Child Support Agency, which takes an active role in facilitating better relations between separating parents.

6 November 2006

⇨ The above information is reprinted with kind permission from the Institute for Public Policy Research. Visit www.ippr.org for more information.

© IPPR

The cost of exclusion

Counting the cost of youth disadvantage in the UK

Unemployment is at its lowest for a generation; more young people are finishing school and going on to further education; and crime figures have stabilised and, in some cases, declined.

Yet there are a significant number of the population who are excluded from this prosperity – who find themselves on the outside looking in. They are often young and live in deprived communities across the UK.

Social exclusion comes with a big price tag – not only for the individual young people who are affected but for their communities and the economy as well. And the costs go beyond the financial: there are also hard-to-quantify costs such as the loss of potential and the long-term, emotional toll of unfulfilled ambitions.

Every day, the Prince's Trust helps 100 more young people gain the skills and qualifications they need to get a job. It gives practical and financial support, developing skills such as confidence and motivation. The Trust works with 14- to 30-year-olds who have struggled at school, have been in care, are long-term unemployed or have been in trouble with the law.

But what is the true value of this transformation to society and the UK economy?

Researchers at the Centre for Economic Performance, London School of Economics, examined trends over time in the UK – comparing them with other similar countries – and, where possible, giving examples of the costs involved. They also looked at the inter-relationship between types of social exclusion.

The Cost of Exclusion reveals that interventions helping young people get into work, stay on in education or avoid crime represent excellent value for money given the measurable costs of social exclusion.

By re-engaging young people and helping them to turn their lives around, this report shows that we can save the UK economy billions each year.

Reducing youth unemployment by one percentage point could save over £2 million in terms of youth crime avoided.

Key findings
The cost of youth unemployment
⇨ The percentage of 16- to 24-year-olds classified as unemployed in 2005 was nine per cent, 8.6 per cent, 10.1 per cent and 6.3

---

per cent in England, Wales, Scotland and Northern Ireland respectively. But in each country and English region the percentage of young people classified as 'not in education, training or employment' (or NEET) is around twice as high.

⇨ Almost a fifth of young people in England, Scotland and Wales are not in education, training or employment. OECD data show that the UK compares very poorly to other countries in this respect.

⇨ The productivity loss to the economy as a result of youth unemployment is estimated at £10 million every day; and this is without taking into account people who are classified as 'inactive' for other reasons.

⇨ There is also a substantial cost to the exchequer of youth unemployment and inactivity: it costs the state about £20 million per week in Job-Seeker's Allowance.

⇨ The personal cost of not being in education, training or employment goes beyond foregone earnings in the longer term: youth unemployment has been estimated as imposing a wage scar on individuals of between 8 and 15 per cent.

The cost of youth crime

⇨ The estimated total cost of youth crime for Great Britain was in excess of £1 billion in 2004.

⇨ The rate of imprisonment is higher in England and Wales than in 12 other European countries. England and Wales also has the highest percentage of prisoners under 18 and the second highest percentage between 18 and 21.

⇨ Prisoners are much more likely to be socially excluded than the general population: they are 13 times as likely to have been in care as a child; 13 times as likely to be unemployed; 10 times as likely to have been a regular truant; and 2.5 times as likely to have had a family member convicted of a criminal offence.

⇨ Within Great Britain, the greatest success in reducing youth crime has been achieved in Scotland. Between 1984 and 2004, success

What is social exclusion?

Social exclusion is about more than income poverty.

Social exclusion happens when people or places suffer from a series of problems such as unemployment, discrimination, poor skills, low incomes, poor housing, high crime, ill health and family breakdown. When such problems combine they can create a vicious cycle.

Social exclusion can happen as a result of problems that face one person in their life. But it can also start from birth. Being born into poverty or to parents with low skills still has a major influence on future life chances.

© Crown copyright

in reducing the number of convictions of those aged 18-21 has been modest for England and Wales. With regards to those aged 10-17, there has been some reduction since 1984. However, there was a partial reversal of the downward trend between the mid and late 1990s.

The cost of educational underachievement

⇨ There has been little change since the mid-1990s in the percentage of young people aged 16-24 with no qualifications. In 2005, these figures stood at 12.6 per cent, 12 per cent, 8.3 per cent and 19.9 per cent in England, Wales, Scotland and Northern Ireland.

⇨ The percentage of young people with low-level or no qualifications in the UK compares very unfavourably to France (for all age ranges) and Germany (for the age range 25-28 and older categories).

⇨ There is some evidence of a relationship between education and health outcomes. And the education of parents can affect the educational outcomes of their children – proof that education can help break the intergenerational cycle of poverty.

⇨ Educational underachievement affects the relative performance of the UK economy. The UK has between 10 and 25 per cent lower output per hour than France, Germany and the US and much of this can attributed to a poorer level of skills and a shortfall of capital investment.

⇨ There is a strong relationship between educational underachievement and crime. US

evidence suggests that social benefits from a one per cent increase in the high school completion rate are equivalent to 14-26 per cent of the private return. Applying these estimates to the UK (with strong caveats) suggests that this might be equivalent to £2-5 billion.

⇨ UK evidence on the effects of the Educational Maintenance Allowance and the Reducing Burglary Initiative suggest that programmes like these can lead to savings of about £3,595-£4,902 per 1,000 pupils because of reduced levels of crime.

April 2007

⇨ The above information is the executive summary of the report *The Cost of Exclusion*, and is reprinted with kind permission from the Prince's Trust. Visit www.princes-trust.org.uk for more information.

© Prince's Trust

⇨ 'Class' is a key issue when attempting to understand why in society certain groups fare better than others. (page 1)

⇨ There is currently no legislation to prevent employers discriminating against applicants on the basis of social class. (page 2)

⇨ Nearly six in 10 adults claim to be working class despite the growth in the number of jobs whose pay and prestige would traditionally be regarded as the preserve of the middle class. (page 3)

⇨ 77% of children with parents in higher professional occupations attained five or more grades A* to C at GCSE, compared to only 32% of those whose parents are in routine occupations. (page 11)

⇨ There has always been an association between health and social class and despite the welfare state and the improvement in health in all sections of societies over the years this discrepancy remains. (page 13)

⇨ Social capital is a term used for how connected people are to their communities through work, family, membership of clubs, faith groups, political and social organisations. (page 14)

⇨ While life expectancy has risen for all social classes over the last 30 years, people in professional occupations (Social Class I) have the longest expectation of life, followed by managerial and technical occupations (Social Class II), and so on. People in unskilled manual occupations (Social Class V) have the shortest expectation of life. (page 15)

⇨ Of those questioned in a *Guardian*/ICM 2007 poll, 89% said they think people are still judged by their class – with almost half saying that it still counts for 'a lot'. Only 8% think that class does not matter at all in shaping the way people are seen. (page 18)

⇨ The new *Middle Britain* report shows that although over half of the population say they are working class (53%), over four in ten Britons (43%) now see themselves as middle class. This is a rise of 44% since 1966, when just 30% of the population regarded themselves as middle class. Moreover, the research predicts that by 2020 more UK adults will regard themselves as middle class than working class. (page 19)

⇨ The *Middle Britain* report indicates a similar level of home ownership between the classes (84% among middle and 75% among working classes) but middle-class homes are worth some 70% more than working-class equivalents. (page 20)

⇨ There was significant structural change in occupational social class during the 20th century. Manual occupations shrank from nearly three-quarters of the workforce in 1911 to around 38% in 1991. They were displaced by growth in managerial, professional and clerical jobs. (page 21)

⇨ Education is the main determinant of whether or not one is upwardly mobile. (page 22)

⇨ In 1964, 47% of people ascribed themselves to a class unprompted, and in 2005 that figure was 45%. Another 47% and 49% respectively did likewise when prompted by the researcher. A minuscule 6% said they did not identify with any class. (page 24)

⇨ An LSE study found that social mobility in Britain – the way in which someone's adult outcomes are related to their circumstances as a child – is lower than in Canada, Germany, Sweden, Norway, Denmark and Finland. Of the countries considered, the US and UK were at the bottom of the mobility league. (page 25)

⇨ The class system is alive and well when it comes to people moving up the housing chain, according to a study funded by the Economic and Social Research Council (ESRC), which talks of 'the tyranny of suburbia'. (page 26)

⇨ New figures from the Office for National Statistics show that household income inequality fell in 2004/5 for the third year running, and post-tax inequality is now back at a level last seen in 1987. Even wealth inequality, which grew substantially over the past decade on the back of house-price increases, has pegged back. (page 29)

⇨ Children who are not in receipt of free school meals are twice as likely to get five good GCSEs as those who are and those from poorer backgrounds are also three times less likely to overcome a dip in their results. (page 30)

⇨ Those from the poorest fifth of households but in the brightest group drop from the 88th percentile on cognitive tests at age three to the 65th percentile at age five. Those from the richest households who are least able at age three move up from the 15th percentile to the 45th percentile by age five. If this trend were to continue, the children from affluent backgrounds would be likely to overtake the poorer children in test scores by age seven. (page 31)

⇨ One in six candidates starting at the UK's top two universities come from just 30 schools – of which just two are state grammars and one is a comprehensive. (page 34)

GLOSSARY

Blue-collar worker

This refers to someone who is in a traditionally working-class job – that is, manual labourers (based on the idea that historically, manual and industrial workers would wear overalls to work which were often blue).

'Chav'

A derogatory slang word, 'chav' characterises a stereotype of a working class youth who dresses and behaves in a certain way. Elements of this stereotype may include Burberry fashion wear, track suits, 'hoodies', baseball caps and chunky jewellery, as well as associations with binge drinking, petty crime and yobbism. Some see the ridicule of the 'chav' and its application to underprivileged young people as an excuse for persecution of the working classes.

Elitism

If something is referred to as elitist, this means it favours the privileged few rather than being based on fairness and equality.

Meritocracy

A system of government whereby positions are gained not through social class or wealth but through individual merit and ability.

'Muddle class'

A term coined in the Future Foundation's *Middle Britain* report to describe the increased confusion over social class caused by decades of social mobility and increasingly complex boundaries between social groups. As traditional class boundaries have become more difficult to define, new social groupings have sprung up, such as ROBs – Rich Ordinary Britons, the 2.67 million people who regard themselves as working class even though their wealth ranks them in the top fifth of the population for assets.

Reverse snobbery

While snobbery is the word used to describe the belief that people belonging to the higher social classes are superior to those belonging to the lower, reverse snobbery characterises the opposite – that is, the scorn displayed towards the higher social classes by the lower. The fact that many more people describe themselves as working class than are defined as such by their occupations could be seen as an example of reverse snobbery.

Social class

Class refers to a hierarchy which exists among social groups in the UK. Traditionally, people belonged to one of three classes – working, middle and upper – based on the status ascribed to them by their occupation and economic position. Massive social and economic shifts in the 20th century led to what many felt was the death of social class, but most would argue that a class system still exists in a different form and is a major part of the collective British consciousness today. It has become a very complex (not to say contentious) issue to define one's social class, factoring in such issues as background and upbringing, accent, manners, culture, education, career and postcode as well as wealth.

Social engineering

Attempting to fix social problems and manufacture a social system to a pre-decided pattern. The Government's aim to get 50% of young people into higher education by 2012, for example, has been called social engineering by critics, who see this as an attempt to force greater social mobility.

Social mobility

The ability of an individual to move around within the class system. In the past, social mobility was an almost unheard-of concept, whereas today we would think little of the daughter of a builder growing up to become an accountant, or a doctor's son forgoing higher education and training as a plumber. However, there are worries that social mobility in the UK has slowed since the seventies and may come to a halt.

White-collar worker

This refers to someone who is in a traditionally middle-class career – a professional, or clerical worker (based on the idea that historically, male office workers would wear a white dress shirt to work).

INDEX

Additional Resources

Other Issues titles

If you are interested in researching further some of the issues raised in *A Classless Society?*, you may like to read the following titles in the **Issues** series:

⇨ Vol. 139 *The Education Problem* (ISBN 978 1 86168 391 5)

⇨ Vol. 137 *Crime and Anti-Social Behaviour* (ISBN 978 1 86168 389 2)

⇨ Vol. 131 *Citizenship and National Identity* (ISBN 978 1 86168 377 9)

⇨ Vol. 130 *Homelessness* (ISBN 978 1 86168 376 2)

⇨ Vol. 115 *Racial Discrimination* (ISBN 978 1 86168 348 9)

⇨ Vol. 112 *Women, Men and Equality* (ISBN 978 1 86168 345 8)

⇨ Vol. 110 *Poverty* (ISBN 978 1 86168 343 4)

⇨ Vol. 107 *Work Issues* (ISBN 978 1 86168 327 4)

For more information about these titles, visit our website at www.independence.co.uk/publicationslist

Useful organisations

You may find the websites of the following organisations useful for further research:

⇨ **Department for Children, Schools and Families:** www.dcsf.gov.uk

⇨ **Economic and Social Research Council:** www.esrc.ac.uk

⇨ **Future Foundation:** www.futurefoundation.net

⇨ **Independent Working Class Association:** www.iwca.info

⇨ **Institute for Public Policy Research:** www.ippr.org

⇨ **Institute for Social and Economic Research:** www.iser.essex.ac.uk

⇨ **Joseph Rowntree Foundation:** www.jrf.org.uk

⇨ **London School of Economics:** www.lse.ac.uk

⇨ **Market Research Society:** www.mrs.org.uk

⇨ **Policy Press:** www.policypress.org.uk

⇨ **Sutton Trust:** www.suttontrust.com

ACKNOWLEDGEMENTS

The publisher is grateful for permission to reproduce the following material.

While every care has been taken to trace and acknowledge copyright, the publisher tenders its apology for any accidental infringement or where copyright has proved untraceable. The publisher would be pleased to come to a suitable arrangement in any such case with the rightful owner.

Chapter One: Social Class

A *level playing field*, © Association of Graduate Careers Advisory Services, *Rise of the working class?*, © Telegraph Group Ltd, *So who do we really think we are?*, © Economic and Social Research Council, *Social class definition*, © Market Research Society, *Class psychology*, © New Statesman, *Middle-class teenagers made 'whipping boys'*, © Telegraph Group Ltd, *Chavs and chav nots*, © Independent Working Class Association / Matthew Holehouse, *A child's-eye view of social difference*, © Joseph Rowntree Foundation, *Health and social class*, © EMIS 2008, as distributed on www.patient.co.uk, *Life expectancy and social class*, © Crown copyright is reproduced with the permission of Her Majesty's Stationery Office, *A question of class – and tomatoes*, © Guardian Newspapers Ltd, *Forget class, it's postcodes that count*, © Associated Newspapers Ltd.

Chapter Two: Social Mobility

Social mobility in Britain, © Guardian Newspapers Ltd, *Middle Britain*, © Liverpool Victoria / Future Foundation, *Social mobility*, © Economic and Social Research Council, *Social contrast*, © Policy Press, *The class debate demands to be heard*, © Guardian Newspapers Ltd, *Social mobility in advanced countries*, © London School of Economics, *The tyranny of suburbia*, © Economic and Social Research Council, *Inequality in Britain*, © Joseph Rowntree Foundation, *The work-rich/work-poor society*, © Institute for Social and Economic Research, *Gap between rich and poor narrows*, © New Statesman, *Education key to promoting social mobility*, © Crown copyright is reproduced with the permission of Her Majesty's Stationery Office, *Social mobility not improving*, © Sutton Trust, *It's official: class matters*, © Guardian Newspapers Ltd, *Keeping class out of the classroom*, © Education Today, *Education is the only way to close class divide*, © Telegraph Group Ltd, *Britain's teenagers' social skills gap widens*, © Institute for Public Policy Research, *The cost of exclusion*, © Prince's Trust, *What is social exclusion?* © Crown copyright is reproduced with the permission of Her Majesty's Stationery Office.

Photographs

Flickr: pages 6 (whiskey kitten); 10 (Daniel Stone); 18 (Francis); 25 (Giuseppe Bognanni); 36 (Jerry Daykin); 39 (ulybug).
Stock Xchng: pages 7 (Renata Jun); 21 (Rafael Velasquez); 28 (Steve Woods).
Wikimedia Commons: page 24 (justinc).

Illustrations

Pages 1, 33: Angelo Madrid; pages 3, 12: Bev Aisbett; pages 15, 29: Simon Kneebone; pages 27, 35: Don Hatcher.

Research by Claire Owen, with additional by Lisa Firth, on behalf of Independence Educational Publishers.

Additional editorial by Claire Owen, on behalf of Independence Educational Publishers.

And with thanks to the team: Mary Chapman, Sandra Dennis, Claire Owen and Jan Sunderland.

Lisa Firth
Cambridge
January, 2008